THE FOUNDING
of
SALEM

CITY OF PEACE

Benjamin W. Shallop

THE
History
PRESS

Published by The History Press
Charleston, SC
www.historypress.com

First published 2022

Manufactured in the United States

ISBN 9781467152136

Library of Congress Control Number: 2022936637

This book is dedicated to the people of Salem, Massachusetts, who inspire me nearly every day with their profound love for and dedication to our shared community, and especially to my wife, Tanya, who gave me the encouragement I needed to finally finish this work. Thank you.

CONTENTS

CONTENTS

INTRODUCTION

On the corner of Washington Square and Brown Street in Salem, Massachusetts, stands what is arguably the least understood monument in America. The monument consists of a large, imposing statue of a stern-looking man wearing a conical hat and clutching a willow bow in his right hand while his left hand is folded beneath a heavy cloak that appears to billow in the wind about him. The statue of the man is perched on a rock and gazes out over the Salem Common, giving the viewer the impression that the man has just climbed that rock to look out on the scene before him, pausing briefly before taking another step. While we have no idea what the man the statue depicts actually looked like, there is nothing to say that it is an inaccurate or misleading depiction. The clothing, a heavy cloak and a wide-brimmed conical hat, is indeed a reasonable assumption of what this man likely wore given the times in which he lived and the work he performed. Unfortunately, this statue has become the victim of the changing perception and nature of Salem over the years. When the monument was first erected in 1913, it sat in front of the East Church, a building that has since become the Salem Witch Museum. Given that the monument also now faces a fairly busy street, few tourists can be bothered to step in front of it and read the bronze plaque on the monument, which reads:

ROGER CONANT
BORN 1592–DIED 1679
THE FIRST SETTLER OF SALEM 1626

I was a means through grace assisting me,
to stop the flight of those few that were then here with me,
and that by my utter denial to go away with them,
would have gone either for England or mostly for
Virginia

Salem residents know this man as Roger Conant, the founder of Salem and the first governor of Massachusetts, but beyond those basic facts, most Salemites know quite little about the man himself or the times in which he lived. Despite the little remembered of this man over the centuries by those who now dwell in the city he founded, nearly every Salem resident is familiar with the experience of cringing a little when they've seen some tourist wearing a chic witch hat point to the statue excitedly and exclaim, "Ooh! That must be the head witch!"

To be fair to those ignorant of the statue's meaning, the story of the first settling of America has been eclipsed by the story of the Pilgrims at Plymouth, and the story of Salem has been eclipsed by the unfortunate events in 1692 known the world over as the Salem Witch Trials. For most of Salem's history, the people of Salem have tried their best to downplay the witch trials and move beyond them. Salem is, after all, historically one of the most important cities in America. It was the first city founded in Massachusetts (Plymouth was not a part of Massachusetts until decades after the city and the colony were founded). The first armed standoff between Massachusetts militia and British Regulars months before the Battles of Lexington and Concord in 1775 occurred at the bridge that spans the North River in Salem. The first naval battle of the American Revolution occurred right off of Salem's shores in Beverly Harbor between a British vessel and a ship that was built in Marblehead, fitted out in Beverly and manned by the men of Salem, Beverly and Marblehead. Salem has periodically served as the capital of Massachusetts and was the birthplace of the China trade, which propelled the young America onto the world scene in the years following the Revolution. In fact, so much trade was carried out between Salem and the peoples of the Pacific Rim that many Indigenous peoples in those regions thought that America must have been a town located somewhere in the nation of Salem. Salem has long been the home of some of America's greatest authors, abolitionists, political leaders and free thinkers. Even today, nearly every merchant, naval and Coast Guard vessel caries a copy of a Bowditch, a guide to coastal navigation developed by Salem's own Nathaniel Bowditch. Salemites have gone on to establish other Salems all across America, and today there is scarcely a state that doesn't have its own

Left: Roger Conant statue. *Photo by Jim Bostick.*

Below: Roger Conant Statue in front of what was once the Second Universalist Church of Salem and is now the Salem Witch Museum. *Photo by Ty Hapworth.*

Salem or New Salem—often even both. Salemites can rightfully boast of the contributions their city has made to America and the world. Some of the most profound have truly shaped the course of history and, more often than not, for the better. Yet for all of these incredible contributions, Salem is forever tainted by the dark days of the witchcraft hysteria of 1692. No matter how hard Salemites have tried to promote other aspects of their heritage, the specter of the witchcraft hysteria has continued to define their city in the eyes of the rest of the nation. In the last decades of the twentieth century, Salem developed an attitude of "well, if you can't beat 'em, join 'em," and turned that international obsession with the Salem Witch Trials into a booming tourist industry.

It is an unfortunate but probably inevitable side effect of the development of witch tourism that has led to so many misconceptions about the statue of Roger Conant over the commons. There is, after all, a giant sign behind him that reads "Salem Witch Museum," and the willow bow, conical hat, stern expression and billowing cloak do look rather witchy. To be fair to the Salem Witch Museum and the international obsession with the Salem Witch Trials, it absolutely *is* a moment in history that should be studied by all lest we should ever repeat it. However, Roger Conant and his early followers were *not* witches—they weren't even Puritans—and they certainly never accused anyone of witchcraft. The men and women who first came to settle at Salem were not stern Protestant reactionaries obsessed with sin who preached fire and brimstone. They were fishermen and the families of fishermen, salters who preserved fish for transport to Europe, and a few farmers, who planted crops to support and sustain those that worked in the fishing industry. The events of the Salem Witch Trials occurred nearly seventy years after they first came to the New World, and Roger Conant and the early settlers of Salem are as far removed from those horrible events as the generation that lived through the Great Depression and World War II are from any current events today.

It is unfortunate that the Pilgrims in Plymouth have so thoroughly placed their stamp over the story of the early settling of New England in the modern popular imagination while the early settlement of Salem has gone largely ignored and forgotten. Plymouth was indeed the first colony to survive a winter in New England, and for that reason alone it deserves much consideration. Yet it must be said that the Plymouth Pilgrim story is not the only story, nor even the most relevant story, about the peopling of North America by Europeans despite being the most widely known. Thus, I have tried to keep the focus of this work away from the Plymouth Pilgrims as much as possible and to focus on them only in the context of what is relevant to the settlement of Salem. This is not Plymouth's story; this is Salem's story and the story of the North Shore of Massachusetts. The result may be rather harsh on the Pilgrims of Plymouth, but the settlement of Salem did in many ways arise out of conflict with them. If you are interested in reading more about the Pilgrims and Plymouth Plantation, I would recommend *Mayflower* by Nathaniel Philbrick or *Of Plymouth Plantation*, a history of that colony written by the governor of Plymouth at that time, William Bradford.

In addition to being a story about Salem and the North Shore of Massachusetts, this is also a story about compromise. The nation that the descendants of these men and women would go on to build is a nation that, despite the rampant violence that defines so much of its history, is one that is truly built on compromise. It was through compromise that interactions between different colonies eventually formed state and federal governments. For all the violence and conflict in American history, what is truly remarkable is that any group of people would ever be able to form any system on which to agree on how to govern themselves. At no time in our history have Americans ever really had completely unifying interests or like-minded moral values. Since its founding, America has been a hodgepodge of competing economic, ethnic, social and religious identities—each of which live, work and struggle to find ways to thrive in the same place. All of this makes one wonder: how is it that there is not complete anarchy? Given all the differences between the competing groups of Americans throughout our history, how is it that any of them could agree on any government?

To answer that question, we have to understand not only the chronological events that led to the establishment of Salem and the Commonwealth of Massachusetts (some of the oldest governmental bodies in America) but also the people who made these compromises and the social, economic, religious, environmental and political forces that drove them to make the choices they did. To understand these, we will first explore the First Nations people of the land we would later call New England in the years leading up to the 1620s. After that, this works investigates the origins of the fishing industry in New England, which brought thousands of West Country Englishmen to the shores of New England, including the first settlers of what would become Salem. It is only after understanding who these people were and what challenges they faced can we appreciate the real significance of the events that led to the founding of Salem. We will explore the working lives of these people as well as their religious and political beliefs. This is not simply a history of the founding of Salem, Massachusetts, this is a history of the *people* who founded Salem.

1

THE NEW ENGLAND THAT WAS

*The Land That Would Later Become New England
and the People Who Lived There*

Here is good living for those who love good fires.
—Francis Higginston, Plymouth Colony, 1624[1]

When Americans of European ancestry today think of the New World at the time of first contact, they often use words like *pristine* or *virgin* to describe the vast forests and landscapes of the North American continent at that time. Such language evokes an image of an untamed land virtually untouched by humanity—and that is indeed exactly how the first European fishermen, traders, explorers and eventually settlers viewed the land. To them, it was a savage place, a dangerous and mysterious new Garden of Eden outside the boundaries of Christendom and civilization. The more religiously minded saw it as a remnant of the world as God had made it, left untouched so that they could try again to hack a living out of it as they believed He had intended. The more commercially minded viewed it as a gold mine with vast and diverse resources to be exploited for both personal and national wealth and glory. Yet to the people already living here, it was a post-apocalyptic wasteland.

When the Italian explorer Giovanni da Verrazzano visited Narragansett Bay in 1524, he described massive canopied forests so devoid of undergrowth that an army could march through them unimpeded. Over one hundred years later in 1634, the colonist William Wood described "in many places, diverse acres being clear so that one may ride ahunting in most places of the land." Account after account of southern New England during this period marvels over vast forests with fantastically tall trees and little if any underbrush. Conversely, northern New England was noted most for its dense forests with think and tangled undergrowth. On the same voyage that led him to Narragansett Bay in 1524, Verrazzano recorded that the forests of the coast of Maine were "full of very dense forests, composed of pines, cypresses, and similar trees which grow in cold regions."[2] Of course, variations in soil quality and climate accounted for much of the diversity between the two regions, yet these natural variations alone do not fully account for the vastly different environments that the Europeans encountered when they first arrived. Native Americans living in northern New England were different from those living in southern New England and interacted with their environment in different ways; likewise, those environments reacted in kind.

On two separate occasions, once in 1605 and again in 1606, Samuel de Champlain visited Cape Ann and left us one of the most detailed narratives of the region and its people prior to the settlement of the area by the English in the 1620s. In July 1605, Champlain wrote:

> *On the 15th of this month, we made twelve leagues. Coasting along the shore we perceived smoke upon the beach, whereupon we approached as close as we could but did not see a single Indian, which made us believe they had fled. The sun was setting, and we were unable to find a place in which to pass the night as the coast was low and sandy* [this was most likely Crane's Beach, Massachusetts]. *Steering south to get away from the land that we might anchor, after sailing about two leagues we perceived a cape* [Cape Ann] *on the mainland to the south, one quarter south-east of us at a distance of some six leagues. Two leagues to the east we saw some three or four rather high islands* [most likely the Isle of Shoals] *and to the westward a large bay* [Ipswich Bay]. *The coast of this bay, ranging around to the cape, extends inland from the place we were about four leagues. It is some two leagues broad from north to south, and three across its entrance. Not discovering any place to anchor, we determined to proceed to the above mentioned cape under short sail for part of the night; and approached to sixteen fathoms of water, where we cast anchor to await daybreak.*
>
> *The next day we made our way to the above mentioned cape, where close to the mainland, are three Islands* [Straitsmouth, Thatcher and Milk Islands] *which are covered with trees of different sorts, like those at Saco and along the whole coast. There is another low Island* [Salvages Island] *upon which the sea breaks, which extends a little*

Insert from Samuel de Champlain's 1612 map depicting Native Americans of the Canadian Maritimes and New England. *Courtesy of the Library of Congress.*

farther out to sea than the others, upon which there are no trees. We named this place Island Cape. Near it we caught sight of a canoe in which were five or six Indians, who came toward us but upon approaching our pinnace, went back to dance upon the beach. The Sieur de Monts sent me ashore to visit them, and to give each a knife and some biscuit, which caused them to dance better than ever. [This beach is now Whale Cove in Rockport, Massachusetts, and notably is no longer wooded, nor does it have a beach anymore.] *When this was over, I made them to understand as well as I could, that they should show me how the coast trended. After I had drawn for them with a charcoal the bay and the Island Cape, where we then were, they pictured for me with the same charcoal another bay which they represented as very large* [Massachusetts Bay]. *Here they placed six pebbles at equal intervals, giving me thereby to understand that each of these marks represented that number of chiefs and tribes. Next they represented within the said bay a river* [the Merrimac River] *which we had passed which is very long and has shoals. We found here large quantities of vines on which the unripe grapes were a little larger than peas, and also many nut trees, the nuts on which were not larger than musket balls. These Indians informed us that all those who lived in this region cultivated the land and sowed seeds like others we had previously seen. This place is at Latitude 43 degrees and some minutes. Having gone half a league we perceived upon a rocky point* [Emmons Point] *several Indians who ran dancing along the shore towards their companions to inform them of our coming. Having indicated to us the direction of their home, they made smoke singles to show the site of their settlement.*

We came close to another little island [Salt Island near Little Good Harbor Beach] *to which we sent out our canoe with some knives and biscuits for the Indians, and observed from their numbers that these places are more populous than others we had seen.*[3]

Champlain didn't stay long at Cape Ann (or the Island Cape, as he called it) during his 1605 visit and never even entered Gloucester Harbor. Instead, he sailed south to explore the region around Cape Cod, which he named "the White Cape." However, he returned to Cape Ann in September 1606, mapped what would one day be called Gloucester Harbor and provided a more thorough description of the area and its inhabitants:

All those Indians from the Island Cape onwards wear no skin or furs. Their clothing was made of grasses and hemp, and barely covered their bodies, coming only down to their thighs. But the men have their privy parts concealed by a small skin. It is the same with the women, who wear it a little lower behind than the men; all the rest of the body is naked.…I saw among other things a girl with her hair quite neatly done up by means of a skin dyed red, and trimmed on the upper part with little shell beads. Some of her hair hung down behind, while the rest was braided in various ways. These people paint their faces red, black, and yellow. They have almost no beard, and pull it out as fast as it grows. Their bodies are well proportioned.

Some of the land is cleared, and they were constantly clearing more in the following fashion. They cut down the trees at a height of three feet from the ground; then they burn the branches upon the trunk, and sow corn between the fallen timber; and in course of time they take out the roots. There are fine meadows for supporting numbers of cattle. This port is very beautiful and a good one, with water enough for vessels and shelter behind the islands. It lies at latitude 43 degrees and we have named it the Beautiful Port [Gloucester Harbor].[4]

Nine years later, in 1614, English explorer John Smith visited the area, and in order to encourage investment in settling, fishing and trading on the coast of New England, he wrote a detailed account of what he found there. While he spoke well of the idea of a potential settlement at

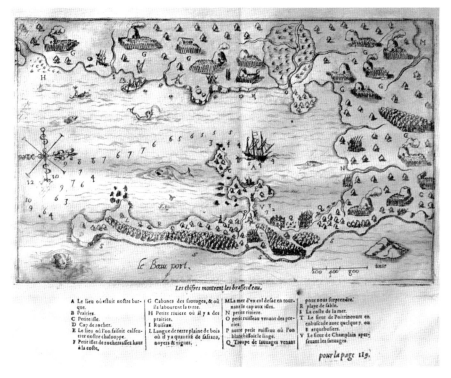

Les chiffres montrent les brasses d'eau.

A Le lieu où estoit nostre bar-
que.
B Prairies.
C Petite isle.
D Cap de rocher.
E Le lieu où l'on faisoit calfeu-
trer nostre chaloupe.
F Petit islet de rochers assez haut
à la coste.

G Cabanes des sauuages, & où
ils labourent la terre.
H Petite riuiere où il y a des
prairies.
I Ruisseau.
L Langue de terre plaine de bois
où il y a quantité de safrans,
noyers & vignes.

M La mer d'vn col de sac en tour-
nant le cap aux isles.
N petite riuiere.
O petit ruisseau venant des pre-
ries.
P autre petit ruisseau où l'on
blanchissoit le linge.
Q Troupe de sauuages venant

pour nous surprendre.
R playe de sable.
S La coste de la mer.
T Le sieur de Poitrincourt en
embuscade auec quelque 7, ou
8 arquebusiers.
V Le sieur de Champlain aper-
ceuant les sauuages.

pour la page 119.

Samuel de Champlain's map of Le Beau Port, modern-day Gloucester Harbor, Massachusetts. *Courtesy of the John Brown Carter Library.*

Cape Ann, he seemed most impressed with the area the Natives called Naumkeag at the base of Cape Ann. Fifteen years later, it would become Salem, Massachusetts:

> *Naimkeck though it be more rocky ground (for Angoam is sandie) not much inferior; neither for the harbor, nor any thing I could perceive, but the multitude of people. From hence doth stretch into the Sea the fair headland Tragabignzanda, fronted with three Isles called the Three Turks Heads: to the North of this, doth enter a great Bay, where we found some habitations and corne fields: they report a great River, and at least Thirtie habitations, doo possese this Countrie. But because the French had got their Trade, I had no leasure to discover it.... The Sea Coast as you passe, shewes you all along large corne fields, and great troups of well proportioned people: but the French having red heere neere six weekes, left nothing for us to take occasion to examine the inhabitants relations, viz. if there be neer three thousand people upon these isles.*[5]

A 1612 map of New France showing the discoveries of Samuel de Champlain. *Courtesy of the John Carter Brown Library.*

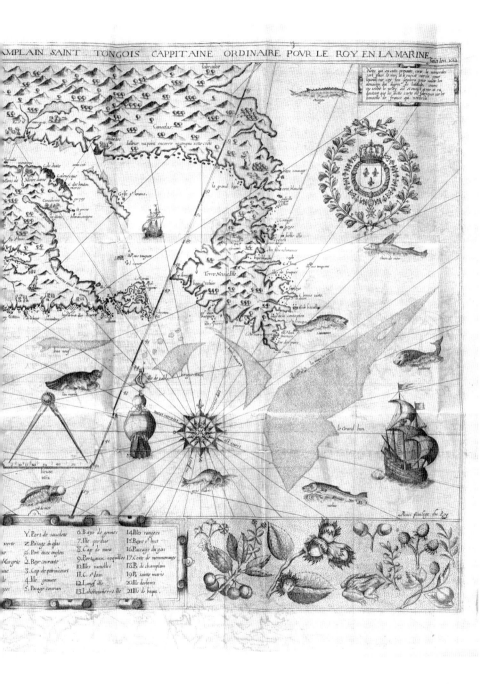

With hundreds of Native peoples around Cape Ann and thousands more around Salem Sound, clearly what is being described by both Samuel de Champlain and John Smith is a region that supported a substantial population, fertile and rich with natural resources. John Smith would even go on to refer to the "Countrie of the Massachusetts" as the "paradise of these parts."[6] In spite of the abundant population present around Cape Ann and Salem Sound in 1614, a decade later, when Roger Conant and the Dorchester Company settled the region, there is no reference given to Native peoples living on Cape Ann and only a small population living in a few fortified habitations around Salem Sound. What happened to those "three thousand people" in the decade between 1614 and 1624?

In 1825, and again in 1835, two large burial mounds in Manchester, Massachusetts, were destroyed to make way for a gravel pit. While no professional archaeological excavation of the site was conducted and we have no way to effectively date the site, a description of what was found there was recorded and eventually passed down to Salem resident and historian Sydney Perley, and that description paints a grim picture. Perley described mounds that were conical, 8 feet high and 160 feet in diameter and surrounded by shallow moats that partially flooded during wet weather. When the excavators dug into the mound, they found "large quantities of bones, but so much decayed that they were cut with a spade or shovel as easily as the ground in which they were imbedded.…The remains appear to have been buried promiscuously and in an erect position, but no Indian implements were found."[7]

While that particular description might not seem so foreboding taken on its own—after all, burial mounds are not all that an uncommon find on any continent—what sets these mounds apart is how strikingly different they are from other burial sites found in the immediate vicinity. Another site in Manchester (also turned into a gravel pit in the nineteenth century) consisted of four bodies, facing west, buried in a circle, with iron hatchets and iron knives and the deceased's heads resting on copper disks. Similar burials of small numbers of people, arranged carefully in a circle, with their heads resting on copper disks and with valued possessions, were found in the vicinity of Waterside Cemetery in Marblehead, Massachusetts, and at Buffrims Field and Forrest River Park in Salem. Clearly, the normal method for people of the region to bury their dead was with a lot of care, ceremony and attention to detail. The presence of the iron tools and other European trade goods in these graves (including Venetian beads in some of the graves in Forrest River Park) shows that this was clearly the practice of these people at the time of contact with Europeans and for some time thereafter, though since these sites were all destroyed well before the invention of carbon dating, we cannot be certain exactly when they were made.[8]

It is unlikely that the Manchester Mounds were constructed prior to the rest of the burials around Cape Ann and Salem Sound. The horrible state of the bones as "so much decayed that they were cut with a spade or shovel as easily as the ground" speaks to this. Obviously, these were bodies buried in a highly acidic soil that led to rapid decomposition; therefore, if they had been much older then they would have likely been in an even worse state. In addition to this, the Manchester Mounds appeared to be hastily constructed. Bodies were heaped on one another and covered with dirt, likely freshly dug from the "moat" that surrounded each structure, with little care paid toward position of the bodies or burial goods. These mounds were certainly not indicative of some carefully orchestrated burial practice like the other burials found in the area. These mounds were built quickly for a rapidly dying people—enough to fill two mounds, each 8 feet high and 160 feet in diameter, that's over 500 square feet filled with human remains.

So what exactly happened to cause such a dramatic decline in the local population in the years just prior to the settlement at Cape Ann? We will never know how many other mass graves like the Manchester Mounds may have dotted the landscape of Cape Ann and Salem Sound prior to the population boom the region experienced in the nineteenth century, but it is likely that other such sites did exist and have long since been plowed over or turned into landfill. It is clear from what limited records and archaeological finds there are that these were trying times for Native peoples of the region. Indeed, it would be no stretch to say that these years were truly apocalyptic for the original inhabitants of Massachusetts. When the Pilgrims wrote of what they found when they first came to New England, they often spoke of God having cleared the way for the settlement of His chosen people, and to be fair to them, that is exactly what it looked like. In 1653, an aging Edward Johnson wrote of his thoughts of that time while relaying some of what he had heard from surviving Natives in southern New England:

> *Even about the year 1618…as the ancient Indians report, there befell a great mortality upon them, the greatest that ever the memory of father to son took notice of, chiefly desolating those places where the English afterwards planted.…Their disease being a sore consumption, sweeping away whole families, but chiefly young men and children, the very seeds of increase. Their powwows, which are their doctors, working partly by charms and*

partly by medicine, were much amazed to see their wigwams lie full of dead corpses, and that neither Squantum nor Abbamocho chould help, which are their good and bad God; and also their powwows themselves were oft smitten with death's stroke. Howling and much lamentation was heard among the living, who being possessed with great fear, oftimes left their dead unburied, their manner being such that they remove their habitations at the death of any. This great mortality being an unwonted thing, feared them the more, because naturally the country is very healthy. But by this means Christ…not only made room for his people to plant, but also tamed the cruel hearts of those barbarous Indians, insomuch that a handful of His people landing not long after in Plymouth Plantation found little resistance.[9]

Thomas Morton, bane of the Plymouth colonists and one of the founders of the ill-fated Wessagusett Colony near present-day Weymouth, Massachusetts, also wrote of this period in his 1637 work *Mourt's Relation*:

The hand of God fell heavily upon them with such a mortal stroke that they died in heaps as they lay in their houses; and the living that were able to shift for themselves would run away and let them die and let their carcasses lie above the ground without burial. For in a place where many inhabited, there have been but one left alive to tell what became of the rest; the living being, as it seems, not able to bury the dead, they were left for the crows, kites, and vermin to prey upon. And the bones and skulls upon the several places of their habitations made such a spectacle after my coming into those parts, that as I travailed in that forest near the Massachusetts, it seemed to me a new-found Golgatha.[10]

Sometime in the years immediately preceding the founding of the Plymouth Colony, a massive outbreak of some horrible European disease had decimated the Native population. It could have been smallpox, measles, the plague or any other number of pathogens unknown to the New World before the arrival of the Europeans. Whatever disease it was, it was most likely introduced by any one of a number of European fishing and fur trading expeditions operating in the region at that time. The Europeans may have seen "this great mortality" as divine intervention, but in reality. that divinity sprang more from the long and horrible history of pandemic and endemic diseases in Europe than any real higher power.

Yet while the decimation of the Native peoples of southern New England was by far the most devastating change to occur for them in the early seventeenth century, it does not fully explain the willingness of the local surviving Native inhabitants to cooperate and ally themselves with the English both at Plymouth and later at Salem during the founding years of both of those colonies and only partially explains the complete lack of any Native presence on Cape Ann during Roger Conant and the Dorchester Company's attempt to establish a settlement there. After all, while both Native peoples and Europeans alike were completely incapable of fully understanding the intricate molecular details of an outbreak of any contagion, Native Americans were certainly aware of the basic observation that when Europeans showed up, a lot of Natives would quickly get sick and die horribly. Rationally speaking, it would have made far more sense to keep Europeans at arm's length and do whatever was in their power to drive the newcomers from their shores. So why then did they partner with them? Native American hospitality? Fear? Another example of the divine hand of God?

The answer is far more practical than any of that. Disease wasn't the only massive transformation wrought on the Native societies of New England during the sixteenth and seventeenth centuries. The influx of European trade goods had also exacerbated existing intertribal conflicts that had left the tribes of southern New England in constant fear of the tribes farther to the north.

By 1600, the tribes of southern New England had developed into fairly settled societies with vague but identifiable borders and fairly routine patterns of subsistence based on agriculture, seafood and game hunting. On what is now Boston and the North Shore of Massachusetts lived the Massachusett (hence the name of the state). To the south of them around Plymouth, Cape Cod and the islands lived the Wampanoag and their kinsmen the Nauset. Rhode Island was nearly exclusively the land of the Narragansett, while southern Connecticut was the home of the Pequot, Mohegan and Mattabasic Peoples. Northern Connecticut and central Massachusetts was the dominion of the Nipmuk, and in the far western regions of Massachusetts around the Connecticut River lived the Pocumtuk. While there were regional dialects as well as alliances and rivalries between nations, these people were fairly similar to one another in their language, lifestyles and political customs. They all grew their corn, squash, beans and pumpkins together in such a complex and perfected manner that each vegetable complemented the growth of the other; they fertilized the soil with fish and hoed it into neat little rows. Nations all seasonally migrated to the coasts in the summer to take advantage of the

Gosnold encounter with Native Americans. *Courtesy of the Encyclopedia of Virginia.*

abundant seafood and, once the harvest was completed, migrated back into the interior to exploit big game and avoid the deadly coastal storms in the winter. They lived in neat villages of small bark huts called wigwams and often surrounded these huts with some sort of palisade for shelter, defense and to keep out wild animals. One such "fort" was located near the intersection of modern-day Humphry and Maple Streets in Marblehead, Massachusetts; it was circular and about fifty feet in diameter, as was another on Castle Hill in Salem.[11]

Collectively, these are the people who turned the vast forests of southern New England into shaded pasture lands with dense canopies of diverse hardwood trees and little underbrush by periodically burning the land so that wild game would flourish. They fished with weirs and dammed ponds to increase fish populations. Much like Europeans, the Native Americans of southern New England had, through these practices, engaged in altering their landscape to maximize that environment's potential to support their lifestyle for thousands of years, and that environment had adapted to them as well. The result was obviously vastly different from the result of the Europeans' interactions with their own environment, but it was in no way less intentional or methodical. It was simply different and, given the size of the populations reported by Samuel de Champlain and John Smith, quite successful for them.

However, their neighbors and distant kin to the north of New England lived a much different lifestyle. Going north up the coast from the land of the Massachusett, we would first encounter the Pennacooks around Portsmouth, New Hampshire, followed by the Sacos, Sheepscots, Androscoggins, Kennebecs, Penobscotts and finally the Passamaquadies near the modern border with Canada. These people, like their cousins to the south, were predominantly Algonquin speaking but lived vastly different lifestyles. The region then, like today, was much more sparsely populated, with a harsher winter, poorer soil quality and far less suitable for agriculture. Thus the natives of northern New England, while engaging in some small-scale horticulture, were far more dependent on hunting and gathering than their cousins were to the south. Yet to the Native peoples of southern Massachusetts, the greatest threat to their survival in the first decades of the seventeenth century wasn't the Europeans or any of these tribes, it was the Mi'kmaq, known to the Native peoples of southern New England as the Tarratine (Algonquin for "Eastern Men").[12]

The Mi'kmaq are the native inhabitants of Nova Scotia and parts of Maine, and many still live in those areas today. Given their geographic location, they were in a prime position to exploit the emerging trade between Native peoples and Europeans during the fifteenth century. For example, there are several documented incidences of Native people, most likely the Tarratine, using small European sailboats known as shallops. Throughout the sixteenth and early seventeenth centuries, the Mi'kmaq enjoyed a lucrative trade with the French for furs in exchange for manufactured goods and firearms. In the second decade of the seventeenth century, the Mi'kmaq began to attack the Massachusett to the south of them devastating efficiency.

Few of the details of what sparked the conflict between the Tarratine and the Massachusett survive; in fact, we cannot even say for certain what years the conflict took place, other than that began in the latter half of the second decade of the seventeenth century. Nearly seventy years after the event, Puritan historian William Hubbard wrote,

> *Those that were seated more eastward…were called Tarratines, betwixt whom and those that lived about Pascatoqua, Merrimack and Agawam… had arisen some deadly feud, upon account of some treachery used by those western Indians against others; so as every year they were afraid of being*

Reconstruction of a shallop, the workboat of seventeenth-century New England, at Gloucester. This shallop is a tender to the *Mayflower* II in Plymouth, Massachusetts. *Photo by author.*

surprised by them, which made them upon every occasion to hide themselves among the English after they were settled in any of those places.[13]

The Tarratine unleashed a campaign of complete destruction on the tribes of Southern New England. Using their newly acquired shallops, the Tarratine soon proved capable of raiding and burning villages as far south as the Wampanoag People. One of those Tarratine raids that struck fear in the hearts of the Massachusett occurred at Naumkeag in present-day Salem, Massachusetts. While the details, including the exact year, of this raid are vague, the repercussions for the Massachusett are well documented. At the time, the sachem, or chief, of the Massachusett was a man named Nanapashemet, whose main residence was at Castle Hill in Salem. Fearing the Tarratine attack on Naumkeag, Nanapashemet moved to the vicinity of present-day Medford, Massachusetts, to escape and was later found by the Tarratine there and killed. Before moving to Medford, Nanapashemet sent his wife and children into hiding someplace farther in the interior of Massachusetts.[14]

It is unfortunate that Nanapashemet's wife's real name has been lost to history. We know her today only as "the Squaw Sachem." Clearly that was not her name, and it must be acknowledged that the term *squaw* is rather problematic. There is a great deal of debate over where the word comes from. It is likely either a French corruption, one of several Algonquin terms for "woman" or a variation of an Iroquoian word for female genitalia. "Squaw" quickly became a word used by Europeans to refer broadly and often derisively to Native American women. The word was definitely not a term a Massachusett woman would have used to describe herself. This is especially true of a woman who was at the time the leader of her people. "Squaw Sachem" was the name bestowed on her by the Englishmen who recorded the history and referred to her in correspondence with other Englishmen. Tragically, her actual name has been completely lost.

There are some other hints about what her name may have been. There is a record of her signature on a document in the collection of the Peabody Essex Museum, but that signature is a drawing of a bow and arrow with the words "The Squaw Sachem's Mark" scrawled next to it by some Englishman. There is also a Native American woman named Sarah Wuttaquatinnusk on the deed for the city of Salem, but that document was signed in 1686, roughly seventy years after the death of Nanapashemet. While it is not impossible that Sarah Wuttaquatinnusk was the same person as the woman who signed her name as a bow and an arrow, it is highly unlikely given the extremely short life expectancy of the time and the fact that whatever her age was when she became the leader of her people, she clearly was an adult with children of her own. At any rate, the woman with the bow and arrow signature returned to Naumkeag, assumed the role of sachem soon after and began trying to rebuild the Massachusett. Shortly thereafter, the English came to settle on her shores. After the Massachusett were so thoroughly decimated by disease and engaged in brutal warfare against an enemy with superior technology, it is no wonder that she viewed these new English settlers as valuable potential allies. Years later, some of Salem's first European inhabitants recalled,

> *When we settled, the Indians never molested us…but shewed themselves very glad of our company and came and planted by us and often times came to us for shelter, saying they were afraid of their enemy Indians up in the country, and we did shelter them when they fled to us, and we had their free leave to build and plant where we have taken up lands.*[15]

Relationships between the Massachusett and the English were not always so benign. When the Plymouth Colony was first established, the Pilgrims entered into a series of alliances with the Wampanoag, Nauset and Narragansett Peoples that often aggravated the Massachusett. At the same time, the Plymouth Colony was facing rival English attempts at settlement and commercial exploitation of resources in other parts of the region. Unfortunately for the Massachusett, this occasionally led to some violent encounters with the Plymouth colonists. Despite these unfortunate events, the Massachusett still welcomed the settlers at Cape Ann and later at Naumkeag (Salem). After all, the settlers at Cape Ann, while still English, were a different people than those at Plymouth—as different from the Plymouth colonists as the Massachusett were from other Algonquin-speaking peoples.

2

THE FISHERMEN

Cod, the Rise of the North Atlantic Fishing Industry and the People Who Worked It

On some unknown day sometime in June 1625, a company of actors gathered on a stage on the shore of Cape Ann. It was no theatrical stage, merely a crude wooden platform covered in split and drying codfish that was built so that it hugged the coast above the water. Nor were these actors assembled that day to perform any of the works of William Shakespeare, George Chapman, Ben Johnson or any of the other popular playwrights of the time. It is likely that no one assembled there that day realized it, but these actors would each play a role in a high drama, the ramifications of which would still be relevant centuries after their deeds that day were long forgotten. On one side of the stage stood a handful of heavily armed men under Myles Standish, the former mercenary turned military commander of the Plymouth Colony to the south. Thirty-one-year-old Standish was an extremely short man. He was often ridiculed about his height by his contemporaries and may well have felt the need to overcompensate for his stature with the acts of bluster and bravado for which he was so well known. Yet while those who disliked him may have snickered at his height, none doubted that he was a deadly and dangerous man. Standish had extensive military experience serving as a mercenary in the religious wars of the early seventeenth century on the European continent and was one of the only colonists in New England to have led a successful expedition against the Native Americans. On that day in June, he would have dressed the part of the military commander with a metal helmet, breastplate and claymore sword at his side—though all of these accoutrements would likely have been somewhat tarnished after five years in the New World.

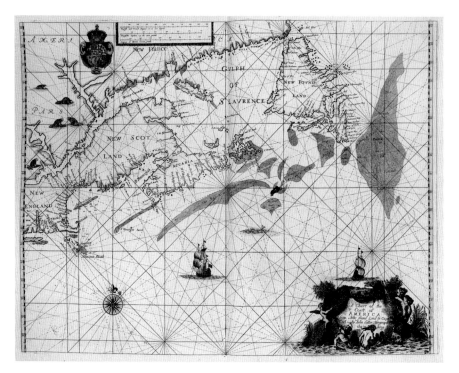

A 1672 chart of New England and the Canadian Maritimes showing offshore cod fisheries. *Courtesy of the John Carter Brown Library.*

On the other side stood a motley collection of fishermen and colonists who that year had been employed in building a new settlement and colony to capitalize on the booming cod fishing industry in the region. Remarkably, given the normal outcome of disputes between rival factions during the early days of the colonization of the Americas, this dispute did not end in violence. Instead, a compromise was reached that would eventually go on to open the door for the founding of the Massachusetts Bay Colony. If Massachusetts was born when John Endicott received a royal charter for Salem, Massachusetts, in 1629, then it was conceived on that day four years earlier at Cape Ann.

Like most whose actions give birth to profound changes that are felt for generations to come, those who labored beneath the massive granite boulder on the gentle slope of the western side of what would one day be known as Gloucester Harbor were much more preoccupied with the task at hand than any airy thoughts of philosophy or politics. On that unknown day, the task at hand was drying and salting codfish. Unlike their belligerent neighbors

A seventeenth-century cod stage. *Courtesy of the John Carter Brown Library.*

to the south in Plymouth, this was not a colony of religious dissidents transplanted across the vast Atlantic Ocean to hack out a community where they could practice their beliefs free of interference from the Crown. The people of the Cape Ann Colony, like generations of New England fishermen before and after them, were here to fish, preserve fish and ship that fish back to markets in Europe. What marked this group as different from the hundreds of fishing and fur trading expeditions before them was that this small workforce was here to stay.

Present that day was one Captain Hewes, who commanded a fishing ship that had just come in with a load of cod and was currently moored in the harbor. There was also present a Captain Pierce of the ship *Anne*, also moored in the harbor. Two other men there that day, John Balch and William Jeffrey, had immigrated to New England earlier to work at a fishing station located near present-day Portsmouth, New Hampshire, and slowly made their way to Cape Ann from there.[16] John Woodbury had been sent out to Cape Ann by his employer, the Dorchester Company, a year or so earlier in an attempt to introduce cattle to the area. Likewise, Peter Palfray had been at Cape Ann for some time already, yet the exact nature of his employment is unknown.[17] A certain Mr. Fells was also present, and he may have migrated to Cape Ann from the Plymouth Colony as a result of unwanted scrutiny over his relationship with a young servant by the governor of that colony, William Bradford. In a letter to the Earl of Arundel the following month, a certain David Thomson claimed to have been present and instrumental in the events that were about to unfold, despite the fact that no other chronicler seems to take any notice of him.[18] Thomas Grey, John Gray and Walter Knight had just recently moved to Cape Ann either from Plymouth itself or from a small trading post and fishing station begun a few years earlier by the Plymouth Colony at Nantasket to the south. Also recently arrived from

Nantasket was the Reverend Lyford; the newly appointed Governor Roger Conant; the governor's wife, Sarah; and their two small children: Caleb, age four, and Lot, who was likely not even one year old. While Sarah Conant remains the only woman we can name, there was more than one woman present in the first year of the Cape Ann Colony; undoubtably, the ratio of women to men was fairly skewed toward the latter.

The object of contention that day was that very same stage on which they now stood. If any description of this particular stage ever existed, then that too has been lost to history. We don't even know how large it was or precisely where it was located on the western shore of Gloucester Harbor, though it would have been situated so that the fish would be exposed to the sun and wind, hanging somewhat over the water to provide easy access to the boats, and offal from the cleaned fish could be easily discarded into the sea. It was likely roughly made of local wood and joined together by handmade pegs and coarse rope given that manufactured goods were scarce and so valued that if anything could be made or maintained with anything else it most certainly was. That stage, saltworks, a clapboard house and "structures usually pertaining to the fisheries" built at the same time are the only buildings for which there is a record, but given that there were quite a few people living, working and traveling to and from there at the time (though the exact number is also unknown), we can be certain that some other structures existed.[19] Yet whatever structures did exist were likely not even of the grandeur of the fishing stage or small clapboard house. Like the nineteenth-century boomtowns of the American frontier, this was a colony of people only just recently arrived for the purpose of staking a claim over part of the trade of a specific marketable resource—in this case codfish and the preserving of codfish. Survival, work and profit were the top priorities, and any housing built at this time would have been haphazard and temporary solutions intended to be torn down or made more permanent later on.

It seems rather trite today that a dispute that began over a small wooden platform would culminate into an armed standoff between two bitterly opposed groups of Englishmen. After all, it was nothing more than an elevated platform of wood, easily assembled nearly anywhere along a vast coastline. There was nothing unique about it, and countless others had been built on rocky inlets and sandy beaches from Cape Cod to Labrador. What made this particular stage unique was that it was part of a permanent settlement, and ownership of that stage represented a claim in both the territory and the anticipated profits to come. That's why Myles Standish

Stage for drying and salting codfish, Newfoundland 1763. It is likely that the stage built at Cape Ann was similar to this one. *Courtesy of the John Carter Brown Library.*

led sixteen or seventeen "Muskateers" from the Plymouth Colony to take possession of the stage, and that's also why when Captain Hewes saw them marching from the beach up toward the stage, he ordered his fishermen to erect a hasty barricade on that very stage to repel them.[20]

THE ENGLISH EXPLOITATION OF the North American cod fisheries, the industry that employed the first English men and women who settled at Cape Ann and later Salem, began well over a decade before Columbus made his famous voyage in 1492. By the fifteenth century, fishermen from Bristol had been plying the North Atlantic to both fish and trade with Iceland for cod for many years. In the 1460s, the Hanseatic League pressured the Icleanders to cease trading cod with the English, and the subsequent lack of trade created a bit of a depression in the port city of Bristol, England. As the once lucrative trade in cod came to an abrupt halt, rumors and legends ran rampant in the port cities of the west country of England about a mystical land far to the west called Hy-Brasil that was abundant in codfish.

Against this backdrop, two men from Bristol devised a strategy to discover and exploit new cod fisheries in the North Atlantic. One was a customs official named Thomas Croft and the other a Bristol merchant named Jon Jay.[21] In 1481, Croft and Jay outfitted two ships, the *Trinity* and the *George*, to go in search of Hy-Brasil and new fishing grounds. While neither Croft nor Jay made any mention of discovering Hy-Brasil, they did turn a healthy profit in dried codfish. Because the two men refused to say where their cod had come from, and because it arrived in Bristol already dried and salted (something that could not be done aboard ship), it was assumed that they were purchasing it from somewhere. Since it was illegal for customs officials to engage in foreign trade, Croft was brought up on charges. These were later dismissed due to lack of evidence when he made the claim that the cod was found somewhere far out in the North Atlantic. Following their efforts, the fishermen of Bristol began to prosper again, so much so that when the Hanseatic League sought to open negotiations on opening Iceland once again to English fishermen in 1490, there wasn't much interest.[22]

Given that English fishermen were being driven farther into the North Atlantic in search of cod by the actions of the Hanseatic League and the desire to turn a profit, and we know that they were trading at least periodically with the Greenland Norse in the years leading up to the dawn of the sixteenth century, it is entirely possible that they were at least periodically fishing off the coast of what would become New England and the Canadian Maritime provinces prior to Columbus's voyage in 1492. It is also possible that they weren't. Either way, it is unlikely that we will ever know for sure. Regardless of who reached North America first, what is undeniable is that English fishermen were gradually spreading out over the North Atlantic during this time and were about to descend on the fertile fishing grounds off the North American coast and likely would have done so completely independent of any voyages of discovery.

On March 5, 1496, King Henry VII of England dispatched John Cabot to explore and lay claim to the northeastern coast of North America.[23] Upon Cabot's return in 1497 and the hero's welcome that he received, Milan's envoy in London, Raimondo di Soncino, wrote a letter to the Duke of Milan regarding the voyage:

> *The Sea there is swarming with fish which can be taken not only with the net but in baskets let down with a stone, so that it sinks in the water. I have heard this Messer Zoane state so much. These same English, his companions, say that they could bring so many fish that this Kingdom would have no further need of Iceland, from which there comes a very great quantity of the fish called stockfish.*[24]

While it is likely that di Soncino was merely simply relaying court gossip to his master (which, to be fair, was one of the primary job functions of an fifteenth-century envoy) and we cannot be certain who this "Messer Zoane" was, one thing is for certain: the court of Henry VII and the merchants and fishermen of Bristol were very excited, to say the least. Henry VII commissioned Cabot for two more voyages of discovery, yet John Cabot—along with his ships, men and two of his sons—never returned from the third voyage.

It is impossible to overstate the importance that cod fishing played in the early exploration, exploitation and settlement of New England. During the sixteenth and seventeenth centuries. the European cod trade was a booming industry for a variety of different reasons, the most notable being the constant need for a stable, cheap and consistent source of easily preserved food to feed the growing poor population of Europe, the slaves on the Caribbean plantations starting to be established and the sailors on the numerous merchant and naval vessels needed to facilitate and protect the rapidly increasing trade between the new world and the old. Additionally, the need for cod was artificially bolstered by the adaptation of Lenten days by the Catholic Church starting in the fourth century. Gradually, the number of Lenten days was increased to every Friday (the supposed day of Christ's Crucifixion and the reason we still enjoy a Friday fish-fry), and by the seventh century, nearly half the days of the year were considered Lenten days. Sex was strictly forbidden on Lenten days, and likewise, red meat was considered a "hot" meat, being red, and was associated with passion and sex. Fish and meat from animals found in the water, on the other hand, were considered a "cool" meat and a perfectly acceptable source of protein on Lenten days. Under English law, the penalty for eating meat on a Friday was hanging, and this law remained in force in England until Henry VIII broke from the Catholic Church in the sixteenth century.[25] However, even after the break with the Catholic Church, the English still continued to impose fines and penalties (though it was no longer a hanging offense) on those who ate red meat on Fridays. By the sixteenth century, the fishing industry had become such a vital economic force in England that in 1563, a bill was presented before Parliament that would have expanded lean days to twice a week by adding Wednesday to Friday. The bill was dropped, however, and soon the Church of England found that selling permits that allowed wealthier Englishmen to eat red meat on Fridays was a profitable source of revenue.

For the rest of Catholic Europe, however, Lenten laws were still strongly in effect, and the need for a cheap source of food for the growing population of poor Europeans, the rapidly expanding shipping industry and later the plantations of the Caribbean was more vital to the English than ever. It is estimated that during the seventeenth century, roughly 60 percent of the fish consumed by Europeans was cod.[26] Of all species of fish, cod (along with haddock and whiting) lends itself well to preservation, because unlike most other species, it is almost entirely devoid of fat. In a time when packing meat in salt was one of the only ways to effectively preserve any source of food for a long period of time, a nearly fatless meat was extraordinarily important. Fat cells resist salt and greatly slow the rate at which salt can permeate the meat, the result being that it is far more likely for fatty meats to spoil and rot before the salt has a chance to adequately set in. The Norse discovered early during the Viking age that cod, unlike oily or fatty fish, can also be quickly air dried, which is an essential first step in the process of salt packing the meat for long-term preservation. As the Norse traded, raided, conquered and colonized throughout Europe, they spread their knowledge of cod preservation wherever they went. Thus, for medieval and post-medieval Europe, the consumption of cod wasn't simply a matter of preference, it was a necessity. This fact was not lost on the English, and they actively set out to control the cod market as much as possible.

Surprisingly, given all of the activity of English fishermen in the North Atlantic in the fifteenth century, the first Europeans on record operating off the coast of what would become New England and the Canadian Maritime provinces weren't English; they were Basque. In 1524, Jacques Cartier, sailing under a commission from the king of France, placed a cross on the Gaspé Peninsula on the south shore of the Saint Lawrence River and claimed the region for France by right of discovery. However, we know that Cartier knew full well that he wasn't the first European to have discovered the mouth of the Saint Lawrence River because he noted in his log the presence of nearly one thousand Basque fishermen already operating in the area when he arrived.[27] Like their English rivals, the Basque had been steadily moving farther into the North Atlantic in search of cod and whales for quite some time. We are not sure exactly where the Basque were getting their whales and fish from prior to 1524, but neither the English nor the Icelanders took much notice of them, and if there is any archaeological evidence of the Basque operating in Greenland or Icelandic waters during the fourteenth and fifteenth centuries it has yet to be found. While they left few records of their voyages, their effect on the region during the sixteenth century was profound.

Throughout the sixteenth century, the Basque began to establish fairly permanent whaling and fishing stations all over the Gulf of Saint Lawrence and Labrador. Twenty such stations built during the middle of the sixteenth century have been identified in the Red Bay region on the southern coast of Labrador alone, with the earliest one there dating to 1543.[28] These shore stations were built as bases for fishermen to dry and salt their cod catch and for whalers to boil down blubber into oil in order to make both products easier to transport across the Atlantic to markets in Europe. While there isn't any evidence of the Basque setting up stations in New England during this period, it is quite obvious that they were at least engaging in trade with the Native populations of the area by the beginning of the seventeenth century. On May 14, 1602, while exploring the coast of New England for the Virginia Company, Captains Gosnold and Gilbert encountered near forty-three degrees north latitude "eight of the savages in one of their *shallops* who boldly came aboard them, which considered with shew that some Biskaners had been trading or fishing there" (emphasis added).[29] That latitude would place the expedition somewhere near the vicinity of Cape Ann, Massachusetts, during this encounter. However, what is most telling about this encounter isn't that Gosnold and Gilbert noted that they believed "Biskaners" had been trading in the area but that the Native Americans they encountered were in a shallop.

A shallop was a small, usually single-masted, vessel with a wide beam and a shallow draft common among various European fishermen during this time. It was easy to assemble, relatively portable on larger vessels and could operate on both the open ocean during calm weather and closer into shore. John Smith used a shallop to explore and chart the Chesapeake Bay in 1607 for the Virginia Company. In short, the shallop was the workboat of choice for European sailors of the sixteenth and seventeenth centuries. Yet like all sailing vessels, shallops took some degree of expertise to handle properly. It is doubtful that someone completely unfamiliar with sailing could just happen upon some discarded shallop and learn how to use it on their own given the complicated rigging of the vessel. The fact that Native Americans possessed enough expertise to actually sail the boat out to meet Gilbert and Gosnold is indicative that there was at least some degree of substantial contact between themselves and whomever they acquired the vessel from.

Nor was this the only recorded incident of New England Native Americans using shallops. On July 31, 1607, an English expedition to establish a colony in Maine on behalf of George Popham (known as the Popham Colony, which was abandoned after one year) anchored off Monhegan Island and noted:

> *We had nott ben at anker past to howers beffore we espyed a* bisken shallop *Cominge towards us havinge in her eyght Sallvages & a Lytell salvage boye they came near unto us & spoke unto us in thear language. & we makinge Seignes to them that they should com aboard of us showinge unto them knyues glasses beads & throwing into thear bott Som bisket but for all this they wold nott com abord of us but makinge show to go from us. We suffered them. So when they wear a Lyttell from us an Seeinge we proffered them no wronge of thear owne accord returned & cam abord of us & three of them stayed all that nyght with us the rest departed in the shallope to the shore makinge Seignes unto us that they would return unto us again the next daye.*
>
> *The next daye the Sam salvages with three salvage women beinge the fyrst daye of Auguste retorned unto us bringing with them Som feow skines of bever in* an other bisken shallop *& propheringe thear skines to trook with us but they demanded ouer muche for them and we seemed to make Lyght of them So then the other three which had stayed with us all nyght went into the shallop and so they depted* ytt Seemth that the French hath trad with them for they use many French word.[30] [emphasis added]

In addition to this encounter, a French Jesuit missionary named Baird traveling up the Penobscot River in Maine in 1611 recorded, "At the

Monhegan Island, Maine. *Photo by author.*

confluence of the two rivers was one of the finest communities of savages I have yet seen. There were eighty canoes *and one shallop*, eighteen cabins, and as many as three hundred souls."[31]

By the first decades of the seventeenth century, West Country English fishermen were operating out of several fishing stations up and down the coast of New England. In Maine alone, twenty separate English cod fishing stations from the 1600s have been identified to date.[32] Beginning in the sixteenth century (and possibly earlier), these fishing stations were intended to be seasonal and developed on a first come, first served basis. Cod fishing was best in the summertime off the Grand Banks of Newfoundland, but in the wintertime, the cod would move closer to shore in the Gulf of Maine to spawn. Thus, fishing in the wintertime was far more common in New England, although some summertime fishing occurred there as well. English captains of fishing vessels would race out of ports in Bristol, Devon, Budleigh and other West Country fishing towns in order to be among the first on the waters off the coast of Newfoundland or New England when the fishing season began. Once on location, they would test their lines in a few locations before settling in and laying claim to a site for the season, and access to the right onshore fishing station could make or break an expedition. Needless to say, competition between the different fishing expeditions over access to the best shore sites was intense and often violent.

Extremely large crews were required for these seasonal fishing expeditions. For one expedition, at least 20 men had to be trained as highly specialized carpenters and caulkers to construct these seasonal facilities on land and make necessary repairs to ships, boats, barrels and more as needed; 60 fishermen would have been required to man the dozen or more shallops that operated out of each fishing ship and actually did the work of laying out the lines and nets to catch the cod. Then, 10 additional fishermen were required to keep the expedition well stocked with bait fish, and 20 men and women were stationed on shore to clean and split the cod for drying and salting. All told, a single sixteenth- or seventeenth-century seasonal fishing expedition could easily include well over 120 people. While records from this period are scarce, it was recorded in correspondence to Robert Gorges (the son of Sir Fernando Gorges and patron investor for many of these seasonal fishing voyages) that from 1614 to 1620, eighty vessels visited Damariscove and Monhegan Islands in Maine on seasonal fishing voyages.[33]

The base camp structures of these fishing stations were temporary, primitive and barely suitable for the long and bitterly cold New England winter. John Yonge, a surgeon aboard the *Marigold* during a seasonal fishing voyage to Newfoundland in 1670, described in detail the process of setting up a seasonal shore station:

> As soon as we resolve to fish here, the ship is all unrigged, and in the snow and cold all the men go into the woods to cut timber, fir, spruce and birch being here plentiful. With this they build stages, flakes, cook room, and houses. The houses are made of a frythe [wattle] of boughs, sealed inside with rinds [bark], which look like planted deal [sheathing] and turfs of earth upon, to keep the sun from raning [ruining?] them. The stages are begun on the edge of the shore, and built out into the sea, a floor of round timber, supported with posts, and shores of great timber. The boat lie at the head of them as at a key, and throw up their fish, which is split, salted, &c.[34]

Other accounts describe seventeenth-century seasonal English fishermen being housed in crude long barracks with walls made of turf, fieldstone and/ or branches and roofed with spare sailcloth. Given that the best months to fish cod in the coastal waters of the Gulf of Maine were January and February, these conditions were far from ideal for surviving the harsh New England winter. January through March is known in New England as a time when the temperature can routinely drop well below zero and stay there for days at a time, and violent coastal storms can erupt quickly, bringing hurricane-force winds, snow and freezing rain. Even in the twenty-first century, these storms are notoriously difficult to predict with accuracy; in the seventeenth century, they would have come with virtually no warning at all. While all of these seasonal fishing stations were located in sheltered harbors, they were still coastal bases and exposed to the worst of the weather that the New England winter could throw at them.

While seasonal fishing voyages from Europe continued well past the seventeenth century (and indeed in many ways are still practiced to this day, albeit with vastly different techniques and technology), by the 1620s, English fishermen were beginning to seek out investors to develop more permanent fishing stations in New England. This coincided with a period where the Crown was seeking to establish some system of property ownership over these new holdings and was in the process of granting titles of vast stretches of coastal New England to various aristocrats (more on this in later chapters). Some of these new lords of New England, such as Sir Fernando Gorges and his son Robert Gorges, took a keen and active interest in developing profitable and permanent fisheries in their new holdings, while others, such as Lord William Sheffield, seemed to take more of an absentee landlord approach and simply sold patents for settlements and fishing rights to whoever had the money to pay. In either case, many of these seasonal fishermen were beginning to take those first steps to becoming permanent settlers.

Permanent fishing stations were soon established up and down the coast of New England from Maine to Massachusetts Bay. Few of these now permanent fishing stations could really be considered new settlements, as these locations had been used seasonally for decades prior to their more permanent occupation. Many of these locations had even likely been occupied year-round as different fishing expeditions periodically operated in and out of these sites, though in the summertime there would have been a much smaller population in the region. Despite this, there really hadn't been much of an effort to build anything permanent on these sites or engage in any real agriculture to support them prior to the 1610s. By the mid-1620s, permanent fishing stations, with local "governors" and a year-round workforce to support offshore fishing, were established at Richmond Island, Monhegan Island, Damariscove Island and Cape Elizabeth, Maine; Portsmouth, New Hampshire (then called Pastaqua); and Cape Ann and Nantasket, Massachusetts.

The life of those on shore was a tedious and hard one to say the least. At the height of the fishing season, shallops from the fishing ships would tie up to the stage while shore workers would haul the cod off the boats using large curved pikes and drop the fish on the stage for cleaning. Cleaning the cod for salt packing required three specialists: a throater, a header and a splitter. The fish would first go to the throater, who, using a long, pointed knife, would slit the fish from the throat to the anus. The header would then take the fish and remove the entrails, carefully separate the roe and the liver (which was used to make cod oil and other products) and break the head of the fish off. Finally, the splitter would then secure the fish by the tail to a batten on the stage, make a large cut along the tail fins and carefully separate the flesh from the spine and ribs. The resulting cut of meat could range in size but would be thin, flat and roughly triangular. This cleaned fish would be tossed through a chute beneath the stage into barrels, which were passed down rollers to another part of the stage, where they would be salted. The fish were laid out on the stage, head by tail to maximize the available space, with the skin side facing down. A thin layer of salt would be spread over them using a flat shovel, then additional fish would be placed on top of them and so on until the entire catch was salted into piles. The fish would remain in these salted piles for a day or two, while the livers were boiled in a nearby vat to extract the oil and the roe would be stored in a salt bin. After two days, the fish was then removed from the piles and rinsed in salt water. Then it was taken to a platform to drain and dry, then to nearby flakes (basically smaller stages that served as drying racks) and periodically rotated to ensure they that they dried thoroughly without cooking in the sun for four or five days. After this initial drying, the fish were then stacked in piles on a nearby beach for roughly two weeks until these piles began to sweat moisture, at which point the piles would be disassembled and the fish reshuffled and stacked into new piles to ensure that moisture remained at a minimum throughout the pile. This beach drying could last for more than a month. Then the fish were placed on stone slabs higher up the beach and pressed with either larger codfish (which was preferable) or other large slabs of stone, the weight of which would squeeze out the last drops of moisture. This would then be covered in sailcloth until it was ready to be packed and shipped back across the Atlantic.

While those employed on land in the cod fisheries of the seventeenth century had a difficult and tedious job, those employed in catching the fish found themselves in near constant danger. Fishing at this time was conducted by stationing the main ship in an area likely to prove fertile and lowering the dozen or so smaller shallops into the water to deploy weighted, baited and hooked fishing nets between them. This required an incredible amount of skill and coordination among the fishing crew and even under ideal circumstances could prove prone to hazard. Yet it must be remembered that for the seventeenth-century fishermen in New England, this work was largely done in the wintertime. Even on calm days, working on the water in the winter is difficult work. Sails and rigging froze along with limbs and fingers if the sailors were not careful. Add to this the ever-present danger of the legendary winter nor'easters for which New England is so well known and one can easily see why even today, fishing is one of the most dangerous occupations there is despite all of our technological advances over the past few centuries.

Whether they worked on the shore or at sea, those who worked in the New England fisheries of the seventeenth century tended to have considerable drinking problems, and this was only confounded by the lack of entertainment while stranded on an outpost during a cruel winter on the far side of the world. Inevitably, employers sought to capitalize on this and developed a system similar to the notorious company stores of the Industrial Revolution. On average, a fisherman could expect to make about ten pounds in a decent season, depending on the size of the catch and the market when they returned home. However, that money wouldn't come in until the ship was paid off. In the meantime, employers would offer alcohol, clothing and other goods on credit to be paid against their future share of the catch. Inevitably, this often left both fishermen and shoremen incredibly indebted to their employers under a system that could aptly be described as wage slavery. Debt servitude was such a profitable enterprise that in some cases a brisk trade developed back in England of merchants and employers trading the terms of now indentured servant fishermen in a manner not all that dissimilar to the modern stock market.[35] John Josselyn, who worked in the fisheries of New England in the early seventeenth century and later wrote an account of it titled *Adventures in New England*, described in detail the lives of fishery workers and their relationships with their employers:

> *The merchant to increase his gains by putting off his commodity in the midst of their voyages, and at the end thereof comes in with a walking tavern, a bark* [a type of ship] *laden the legitimate blood of the rich grape, which they bring from Phial, Madera, Canaries, with Brandy, Rum, and Barbados strong-water, and tobacco, upon coming ashore he gives a taster or two, which so charms them…for two or three days, nay sometimes*

a whole week till they are wearied from drinking, taking ashore two or three hogshead of wine and rum to drink off when the merchant is gone.… When wine in their guts is at full tide, they quarrel, fight, and do one another mischief, which is the conclusion of their drunken computations. When the day of pay comes, they may justly complain of their costly sin of drunkenness, for their shares will do no more than pay the reckoning; if they save a kental or two to buy shoes and stockings, shirts and waistcoats with, 'tis well, other ways they must enter into the Merchants books for such things as they stand in need of, becoming thereby the merchant's slaves, & when it riseth to a big sum are constrained to mortgage their plantation if they have any, the merchant when the time is expired is sure to seize upon their plantation and stock of cattle, turning them out of house and home, poor creatures, to look out for new habitations in some remote place where they can begin the world again.[36] [It should be noted that the term plantation simply meant any landholding of any size during this time.]*

There is no doubt that the constant cold, stress, uncertainty, boredom and loneliness of the realities of working in a New England fishery during this period greatly contributed to the rampant (and disturbingly profitable) alcoholism of the men who made a living there. Like any people far removed from their homes in a strange, cold new place and facing constant danger, these early New England fishermen were extremely superstitious and clung to some of the ancient beliefs and customs of their motherland. While Protestantism and Catholicism were battling over which would reign supreme over the Church of England, these fishermen stubbornly continued to practice their religion in a somewhat more traditional manner—much to the frustration of their later neighbors to the south, the Pilgrims of the Plymouth Colony. Phineas Pratt, who came to New England around 1623, eventually settled in Plymouth, and he traveled frequently to the fishing stations of Damariscove and Monhegan Island, remarking that upon his arrival at Damariscove, "The men there that belong to the ship, there fishing, had newly set up a maypole and were very merry." Maypoles are part of an early pre-Christian pagan tradition of May Day festivals, tolerated by the both the Catholic Church and at times the Church of England (depending on the reigning monarch) but vehemently opposed by the Protestant reformers. Extreme Protestants viewed the maypole as heathenism, worse than popery in their eyes. To sixteenth- and seventeenth-century Protestants, maypoles and other traditionally pagan beliefs that had been adopted by Christianity were something that needed to be destroyed. William Bradford, the Pilgrim governor of the Plymouth Colony, provided us with a fairly accurate (if somewhat condescending) description of a maypole celebration. In 1628, when indentured servants from the Plymouth Colony left the colony and relocated toward the area of modern-day Quincy, they erected a maypole to celebrate their new freedom from their Pilgrim masters. Bradford described the celebration thus:

> *They also set up a May-pole, drinking and dancing about it many days togaether, inviting the Indean women, for their consorts, dancing and frisking togither, (like so many fairies, or furies rather,) and worse practises. As if they had anew revived & celebrated the feasts of the Roman Goddes Flora, or the beasly practises of the madd Bacchinalians. Morton likwise (to shew his poetrie) composed sundry rimes & verses, some tending to lasciviousnes, and others to the detraction & scandall of some persons, which he affixed to this idle or idoll May-polle. They changed also the name of their place, and in stead of calling it Mounte Wollaston, they call it Merie-mounte, as if this joylity would have lasted ever.[37]*

Despite the myriad hardships and difficulties facing early New England fishermen, the cod fisheries of New England were proving more and more profitable every year to those investors back in England, and every year more and more ships came. Although financial disaster could still easily ruin both an investor and a fisherman if a ship was lost, a cargo spoiled or if one of the many periodic European wars erupted across the Atlantic and closed down a market to codfish, the permanent fishing stations were turning an incredible profit. As the profits of the fisheries began to soar, more permanent settlement in the region began to appear lucrative to various merchant investors in England. Attempts at colonizing in the region had failed in 1607 and 1610, but by the close of the second decade of the seventeenth century, several permanent outposts dotted the coastline, and more would be established throughout the 1620s. Slowly, over several decades, the English had developed a permanent and dominant economic presence in the region nearly free of foreign competition, save for the occasional inconsequential clash with their French rivals in the region. Large scale settlement was now inevitable, though by whom and when was still very much in question. Yet, while these fishermen were indeed the first Europeans to populate the region, events in England would soon propel other Englishmen to seek out the region to build a new home and a new England.

3

NEW ENGLAND BEFORE SALEM

*Lords, Lawyers, Tribes, Pilgrims, Strangers and the Legal
Wrangling and Conflict over the Settling of New England,
1620–1623*

B y 1623, around the time the future governor of the Cape Ann
Colony Roger Conant first came to settle in New England, there
were four English settlements in New England. Only one of those
settlements could really be called a settlement. Plymouth was settled in late
1620 and had soon afterward established a trading post/fishing station at
Nantasket, and another trading post/fishing station had been established
by a different company at Piscataqua near present-day Portsmouth, New
Hampshire. Yet the settlement that would cause the most headache for
both the Massachusett and the Plymouth colonists in those early years was
an often-forgotten settlement that didn't even last a full year, Wessagusett,
near present-day Weymouth, Massachusetts. To fully understand why the
Wessagusett settlement was so problematic for the region, we have to first
understand under what authority these settlement expeditions operated and
the tenuous legal footing the Plymouth Colony stood on.

Prior to 1606, trade and fishing expeditions to the New World from
England were chaotic to say the least. England and France both had claims
over the region, but neither had developed any settlement or fortification
to enforce those claims. At the time, European nations operated under the
principle that "all a man sailed by or saw was his own"[38] when claiming
ownership over a newly discovered land. None paid too much heed to any of
the existing territories and claims of the Indigenous peoples except in cases
where it served the European power's interest. Meanwhile, independent

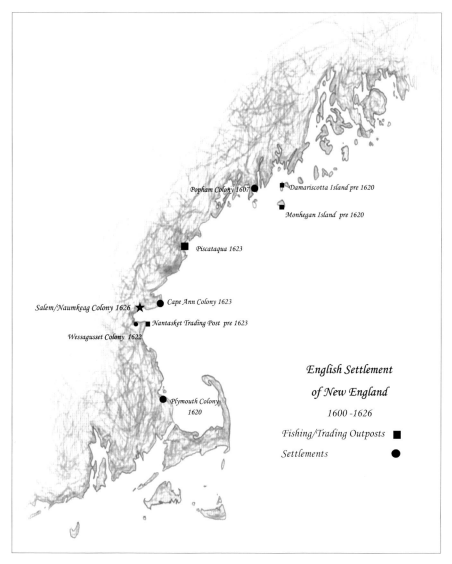

Map showing English settlement of New England, 1620–26. *Map by Justin Patterson.*

traders, whalers and fishermen were prowling the coasts in search of whatever commodity they could turn a profit on. These expeditions, as discussed earlier, cared little about nationality or national claim to a region and hailed from nearly every coastal country of western Europe. Money was obviously there to be made in America, and whichever nation could establish a settlement with a legal claim and defend it would reap the greatest reward.

Establishing a settlement was an extremely costly and dangerous endeavor. There had been several attempts to do so in North America prior to 1600, and nearly all had ended disastrously. The one exception was the Spanish settlement at Saint Augustine, Florida. However, Saint Augustine wasn't truly a settlement and wouldn't turn a profit for the Spanish government for a long time. Instead, Saint Augustine served primarily as a military outpost to provide a safe harbor for the Spanish treasure fleets sailing out of Mexico and the Caribbean and thus only really existed thanks to massive investment on the part of the Spanish government. Other attempts at settlement by the Spanish, English and French in the region had been colossal failures in both money and lives lost. While every crown in Europe recognized the potential of the New World, they weren't all that willing to either fund or recruit an expedition for permanent settlement.

In 1606, James I of England granted the first corporate association for the colonization of North America in order to encourage private investment in settlement schemes. The association consisted of two councils, one in London and one in Plymouth, England, operating under one patent. Each council is often referred to as a "company," but such a term is misleading. Since both councils were operating under one patent, at this time they constituted one entity with separate jurisdictions. During this time, the English referred to the entire Eastern Seaboard of North America as "Virginia," with the London Council governing the settlement of "Southern Virginia" (those parts south of Long Island) and the Plymouth Council governing the settlement of "Northern Virginia" (north of Long Island).[39] According to the 1606 charter, each council was given

> For Us, our heirs, and Successors, GRANT and agree…and they shall and may begin their said first plantation and habitation, at any Place upon the said coast of Virginia or America where they shall think convenient…and that they shall have all the lands, woods, soil, grounds, havens, ports, rivers, mines, minerals, marshes, waters, fishings, commodities, and hearditaments whatsoever, from the said first seat of their plantation and habitation by the space of fifty miles of English statute measure, all along the coast of Virginia and America…with all the islands over within one hundred miles, directly over the said sea coast…and shall and may inhabit and remain there, and shall and may fortify and build within the same, for their better safeguard and defense, according to their best discretion and the discretion of the council of that colony. And that no other of our subjects shall be permitted or suffered to plant and inhabit behind, or on the backside of

them, towards the mainland, without the express license or consent of the council of that colony....

Provided always, and Our Will and Pleasure herein is, that the plantation and habitation of such of the said colonies, as shall plant themselves, as aforesaid, shall not be made within one hundred like English Miles of the other of them.[40]

In addition to lands, resources and settlements, each council was granted extensive rights to govern colonies, including the right to "assign all lands, tenements, and hereditaments, which shall be within the precincts limited to that colony," as well as the right to mint coinage, licenses to transport colonists and materials, seize anyone trafficking goods along the coast and govern these colonies so long as those laws did not conflict with English Common law. In exchange for these rights and the protection of the Crown, these councils were expected to "yield unto Us, Our heirs and successors, the fifth part only of all the same Gold and Silver, and the fifteenth part of all the same Copper, so as to be gotten or had."

While all of this probably sounded quite thorough and grand in the drawing rooms of the court of James I, the reality of what would be needed to colonize the Eastern Seaboard was something completely different. Maps were incomplete and inaccurate, longitude was only a theory and latitude was not an exact science during this time. It must be noted that if the Crown sincerely believed that it would be able to receive revenue from the colonies through the exploitation of mining precious metals like gold, silver and copper as the Spanish had, then it was soon to be greatly disappointed.

Still, this charter did provide the legal protections and potential for profit needed in order to entice investment in colonial expeditions, and two expeditions set sail in 1607. One of them was bound for what is now Virginia and settled at Jamestown, and the other reached what is now Maine on the Kennebeck River. The Maine expedition was chiefly organized by Francis Popham and is remembered by history as the Popham Colony, although the settlement was known as the Sagadahoc Colony. (As mentioned earlier, this was one of the expeditions that encountered Native Americans using shallops off Monhegan Island.) Popham's colonists were far better prepared than their compatriots at Jamestown and suffered a much lower death rate the first year despite the brutal Maine winter. However, when resupply ships came the following spring, they brought the devastating news of the death of Francis Popham. Given the uncertain future of financial investment in the colony without Popham at the helm, some difficulty with the local Natives and the sheer unexpected brutality of the Maine winter, the remaining colonists decided to abandon the colony and returned to England. However, when they left, they sailed in the first ship ever built by Europeans in North America, the *Virginia*. Thus began Maine's phenomenal shipbuilding industry, decades before there was any permanent settlement in Maine. The *Virginia* would go on to serve as a supply ship for its sister colony.[41]

Over the next thirteen years, the Plymouth Council for Northern Virginia essentially lay dormant as a result of extended legal infighting between investors and board members while the London Council for Southern Virginia continued to expand despite massive losses in both lives and capital. Eventually, the corporation would completely split, with the Southern Virginia Council becoming the Virginia Company and the Northern Council becoming the Council of New England (as the name New England had become increasingly popular for the region thanks to the writings of John Smith). It was during this period of extensive legal infighting that one Thomas Weston began making overtures to a certain group of English religious exiles then living in Leyden, Holland, that history remembers as the Pilgrims.

The Pilgrims were the theological descendants of a radical Puritan sect that emerged in the sixteenth and early seventeenth centuries known as "The Brownists" after one of the early leaders of the separatist movement, Robert Browne. While the Pilgrims of Plymouth always vehemently denied any association with Robert Browne, there can be no question that their belief in the need for a complete separation of the Church from the Crown, along with their later exodus to Holland and then North America, had its origins in the Brownist movement.

Whereas the Puritans believed that the Church of England needed to be reformed (or "purified") into a more Protestant church, the Brownists took the radical stance that the Church should be completely separate from the Crown. Robert Browne began his religious career as the domestic chaplain for the Duke of Norfolk. In June 1571, Robert Browne was one of a handful of Puritan clergy who signed a letter to the Archbishop of Canterbury stating their willingness to live peacefully so long as they could practice their faith as they saw fit. The Archbishop of Canterbury responded by stating that they must all adhere to the requirements of the queen's church or be deprived of their livelihoods. As the personal chaplain of the Duke of Norfolk (who was staunch but practical Puritan), Robert Browne did not face the same consequences as the other clergy who signed the letter. It was easier for Browne to preach his faith as he saw fit and, for the most part, keep it under the nose of the Church authorities.

In 1580, Parliament passed an act titled "An Act to Retain the Queen's Subjects in their due Obedience." During this period, the monarchs of Spain, France and Scotland were all using Catholic priests and Jesuit missionaries to foment unrest and undermine the reign of Elizabeth I. However, while this act was designed to root out Catholic rebellion, Elizabeth I was determined that it would apply to her Protestant subjects as well. The act declared, among other things, that

> all persons that do not come to church or chapel, or other place where common prayer is said, according to the Act of Uniformity, shall forfeit twenty pounds per month to the Queen, being thereof lawfully convicted, and suffer imprisonment until paid. Those that are absent for twelve months shall, upon certification made thereof into the King's Bench, besides there former fine, be bound with two sureties, in a bond of two hundred pounds, for their good behavior. Every schoolmaster that does not come to common prayer shall forfeit ten pounds per month, be disabled from teaching school, and suffer a year's imprisonment.[42]

While obviously intended to be used as a tool to suppress Catholicism in England, the insistence on attending the services of the Church of England equally applied to the Puritans as well. Several Puritans were imprisoned and fined. During this period, Robert Browne led a small congregation of devout Puritans to establish a new parish in Zeeland, Holland, and began to openly preach for a full separation from the Church of England. Browne and his followers denied that the Church of England was indeed a true church or that its ministers had been lawfully ordained in the eyes of God. They decried the church as both popish and anti-Christian and declared all its ordinances and sacraments to be invalid. They strictly forbid their adherents to join in prayer or communion with the Church of England or any other reformed Protestant church unless the teachings of those churches strictly coincided with their own. The structure of the Brownist church was, like the Pilgrim and Puritan churches of New England in the following decades, democratic in appearance. Church officers were elected from the parishioners to conduct various services and could subsequently be removed by a vote of the parishioners. When they gathered to warship, members would make a public confession of their faith and would later sign a covenant to guide one another through the teachings of the Gospel as had been agreed to by their elected church superiors.[43]

By the 1610s, the Pilgrims, who referred to themselves simply as the "Leyden Congregation," had for some time been exploring the option of settling somewhere in the New World and had been trying to seek out both the means to do so and a suitable location. Yet putting their plans into practice had become increasingly frustrating given the intricacies and infighting of colonial endeavors during this time. They had even gone so far as to entertain settling under a Dutch patent rather than an English one— that is, until Thomas Weston, an ironmonger from London who dabbled in what we might today call venture capitalism, arrived in Holland. William Bradford, later governor of the Plymouth Colony and historian of their first few decades in North America, recalled,

> *About this time* [late 1610s] *whilst they were perplexed with the proceedings of the Virginia Company...one Mr. Thomas Weston, a merchant of London came to Leyden about the same time (who was well acquainted with some of them* [the Virginia Company] *and a furtherer of them in their formal proceedings)...persuaded them to go on (as it seems) and not to meddle with the Dutch or too much depend on the Virginia Company. For if that failed, if they came to resolution, he and such merchants as were his friends, together with their own means, would set them forth; and they should make ready and neither fear want of shipping or money; for what they wanted would be provided.*[44]

This mysterious angel investor seemed to be the answer to the extremely pious Pilgrims' prayers. Money, ships, provisions and, most importantly a patent with legal authority to send the congregation off to found their New Jerusalem in a New World all appeared at the needed moment, when their faith in their ability to put this endeavor together was being tested. Indeed, Thomas Weston was able to help arrange all of this for the Pilgrims—though perhaps not quite as they had envisioned.

Throughout 1619, Thomas Weston worked with the Leyden Congregation and investors (who at the time were referred to as "Merchant Adventurers" or just "Adventurers") in London to reach an agreement that would outfit and fund the expedition. One of his main goals during this time appears to have been to try to get a fishing monopoly for the colonists over the coastal waters of New England in order to guarantee the financial stability of the colony, but he was unable to achieve this end. All seemed to be going according to plan, and the Leyden Congregation began to settle their estates and sell off their property in preparation for the voyage. William Bradford sold his home in 1619. Then in 1620, right before the voyage, Thomas Weston dropped the bombshell. Claiming that the London investors would not support the voyage unless certain provisions were agreed to, he presented the Leyden Congregation with a new agreement that, given that those of the Leyden Congregation traveling on the first voyage had already sold off so much of their property, they had little choice but to agree with. William Bradford recorded the agreement as follows:

Anno 1620 July 1,

The Adventurers [meaning the investors in London] *and Planters* [meaning the Colonists] *do agree that every person that goeth being aged 16 years and upward, be rated at £10, and £10 to be accounted a single share.*

That he that goeth in person, and furnish himself out with £10 either in money or other provisions, be accounted as having £20 in stock, and in the division shall receive a double share.

The persons transported and the Adventurers shall continue their joint stock and partnership together, the space of seven years (except some unexpected impediment do cause the whole company to agree otherwise) during which time all profits and benefits that are got by trade, traffic, trucking, working, fishing, or any other means of any persons, remain still in the common stock until the division.

That at their coming there, they choose out such a number of fit persons as may furnish their ships and boats for fishing upon the sea, employing the rest in their several faculties upon the land, as building houses, tilling and planting the ground, and making such commodities as shall be most useful for the colony.

That at the end of seven years, the capital and profits, viz the houses, lands, goods, and chattels, be equally divided betwixt the Adventurers and Planters; which done, every man shall be free from other of them of any debt or detriment concerning this adventure.

Whosoever cometh to the colony hereafter or putteth any into the stock, shall at the end of seven years be allowed proportionalbly to the time of his so doing.

He that shall carry his wife and children, or servants, shall be allowed for every person now aged 16 years and upward, a single share of the division; or if he provide them necessaries, a double share; or, if they be between 10 year old and 16, then two of them to be reckoned for a person both in transportation and division.

That such children as now go, and are under the age of 10 years, have no other share in the division but 50 acres of unmanured land.

That such persons as die before the seven years be expired, their executors to have their part or share at the division, proportionably to the time of their life in the Colony.

That all such persons as are of this colony are to have their meat, drink, apparel, and all provisions out of the common stock and goods of the said colony.[45]

According to William Bradford, this differed from the original agreement in two significant ways: first, that after seven years all property and improvements should solely be owned by the planters, and second that each planter should have two days per week for their own private employment and use. In addition to this, the Leyden Congregation had to accept the presence of several additional colonists, various skilled tradesmen and their families that had been recruited by the London Adventurers due to the lack of confidence the Adventurers had in the congregants' ability to perform any profitable work. To say that these other colonists were only grudgingly welcomed by the Leyden Congregation is an understatement, as those members of the Leyden Congregation would refer to them as "strangers" in all of their writings.

The provisions of this agreement would come to play a significant role in propelling the Plymouth colonists into conflict with the Cape Ann colonists five years later. The provision that emphasizes fishing, and Thomas Weston's attempts to secure a monopoly on fishing for the colony, illustrate that this activity was seen as the most likely endeavor to turn a profit for the investors in the colony. Setting up a prosperous fishing operation was listed not only as a priority and obligation on the part of the colonists, but also the placement of that provision prior to even the construction of housing shows how vital the Adventurers viewed this operation. Obviously, both the colonists and the Adventurers were optimistic about finding other sources of revenue and commodities to exploit, but fishing was considered the guarantee of a sound return on an investment. By dividing housing and improvements between the Adventurers and the colonists equally at the end of seven years, added pressure was placed on the colonists to make a profit during that time. Those of the Leyden Congregation in particular, but even the "strangers" as well, were not crossing the North Atlantic to hack out a living in an unknown world just to end up as tenants to absentee merchant landlords in London.

At the same time, it is highly doubtful that the Adventurers in London had any desire to use such property for themselves, excepting as a source of rent revenue perhaps. What seems likely is that those London Adventurers planned to sell this property, property that would be built chiefly out of raw materials harvested near their location, back to the colonists at the end of the seven-year contract. The Plymouth colonists, Pilgrims and Strangers alike, had just seven years to figure out how to survive, turn a profit and then buy back what they would have already purchased by the blood, sweat and tears of their own sacrifice.

Unfortunately, the legal headaches for the Plymouth colonists were far from over when they agreed to the London Adventurers' provisions and finally set sail in September 1620. By the time the expedition embarked, what was formerly the Council of Northern Virginia was still in the throes of much legal wrangling between its investors and board members. Thus the London Adventurers received a patent to settle in the New World from the Virginia Company. On February 2, 1620, a friend of Thomas Weston's named John Pierce was able to obtain a patent for a "Particular Plantation" from the Virginia Company. The exact text of this patent, known as "The First Pierce Patent," no longer survives. However, on the same day that the Virginia Company issued this patent to John Pierce, the company also passed an extremely liberal ordinance for governing "Particular Plantations," which granted leaders associated with "divers of the gravest and discreetest of their companies" nearly complete autonomy within the geographic area outlined under the Virginia Patent. It appears at this time that the Virginia Company was trying to encourage other plantations and settlements in the region it governed and inclined to loosen regulation and authority in order to make prospects for investment and settlement more appealing. However, the jurisdiction of the Virginia Patent ended just north of Long Island. This was of little concern to the colonists aboard the *Mayflower* as it plodded across the North Atlantic in the autumn of 1620, because they had in mind as a destination and a settlement something near the Island of Manhattan at the mouth of the Hudson River. This location, while well north of the settlements of the Virginia Company, was still clearly within the confines of that company's patent jurisdiction and was known to have river access to the interior, a good harbor and near enough to the New England fishing grounds to assume that a good profit might still be made from engaging in that industry.

History may have played out quite differently had everything gone as planned on the *Mayflower* voyage, but unfortunately for the colonists it didn't. As could well be expected in a ship packed with people from diverse backgrounds, tensions on the voyage ran high between the Leyden Congregants, the Strangers and the crew. When they finally reached the New World on November 9, 1620, they were well north of their intended destination off the coast of Cape Cod. After trying unsuccessfully to maneuver through the uncharted shoals on the eastern shore of that promontory, and with it being so late in the season and the captain and crew all too eager to ditch their human cargo and return home, they decided instead to search for a suitable settlement someplace on western side of Cape Cod in Massachusetts Bay. On December 21, they found a suitable harbor to begin their settlement. If they had sailed just a little farther north, they would have discovered the Shawmut Peninsula, the site of present-day Boston, and one of the greatest natural harbors in the Northeast. The fact that they stopped searching at the first decent harbor they found shows how desperate their situation was. Though in their immediate desperation they cared little at the time, the location of the settlement was clearly outside of the bounds of their patent and was for all intents and purposes therefore illegal.

While the *Mayflower* was closing in on the coast of North America, back in England the Plymouth Council of Northern Virginia was beginning to settle and sort its affairs. In March 1620, Sir Fernando Gorges, who had been a major driving force behind the 1607 attempt to establish the Popham Colony and was a prominent member of the Plymouth Council, petitioned James I for a fishing monopoly over New England. James I finally placed his seal on the charter on November 2, 1620, while the *Mayflower* was at sea. A new corporation called "The Council Established at Plymouth in the County of Devon for the planting, ruling, ordering, and governing of New England in America" was born. The Plymouth Council, as it was called for short, had been granted jurisdiction over all of America between forty and forty-eight degrees north and from the Atlantic to the Pacific—wherever the latter would be.[46] Obviously, this overlapped considerably with the Virginia Company patent, but as the actual settlements of Virginia were so far removed from their northern border, it wasn't considered all that much of a pressing issue. However, to say that this placed the Plymouth Colony (which once again had received its "particular" patent under the Virginia Company) in an even more legally awkward situation is an understatement.

Yet the fact remained that in 1621 the Plymouth Colony was the only English settlement in the Northeast, and that gave the colonists, and their investors, a considerable amount of bargaining power. The following summer, on June 1, 1621, John Pierce was able to obtain what would come to be known as the Second Pierce Patent, which read as follows, in part:

This Indenture made the First Day of June 1621,

And in the yeeres of the raigne of our soveraigne Lord James by the Grace of God King of England, Scotland, France and Ireland, defender of the faith et cetera. That is to say of England France and Ireland the Nyneteeth and of Scotland the fowre and fifth.

Betwene the President and the Counsell of New England of the one partie and John Pierce citizen and clothworker of London and his Associates of the other partie Witnesseth that whereas the said John Pierce and his Associates have already transported and undertaken to transport at their own cost and chardges themselves and dyvers persons into New England and there to erect and build a Towne and settle dyvers Inhabitants for the advancement of the general plantacon of the Country of New England Now the sayde President and Counsell in concideration thereof and for the furtherance of said plantacon and incoragement of the said Undertakers have agreed to graunt assign allot and appoynt to the said John Pierce and his associates and every one of them his and their heirs and assignes one hundred acres of grownd land for every person to be transported….with Liberties pryviledges proffites and coomdyties as the said Land and Ryvers which they shall make choyce of shall yield together with free libertie to fishe in and upon the coast of New England and in all havens portes and creekes.…

The said President and Councell aforesaid to gran unto the Undertakers [meaning the London Adventurers] *their heirs and assigns fifteen hundred acres of Land more over and above the aforesaid proporcon of one hundred the person…*

Within Seven Yeeres now next coming, shall and will by their deede intended and under the Common seale graunt infeorre and confirme all and every said to sett out and bownded as aforesaid to the said John Pierce and his Associates…and shall also…graunt unto them…Letters and Grauntees of Incorporacon…with libertie…to make orders Lawes Ordynances and Consitucons for the rule of government.…

In witnes whereof the said President and Counsel have to the one part of this present indenture sett their seals And to th'other part hereof the said John Pierce in the name of himself and his Associates have sett to his seale geven the day and yeeres above written.

[Signed] *Lennox Hamilton, Warwick Sheffield, Fernando Gorges*[47]

Through the Second Pierce Patent, the Plymouth colonists had gained the right to remain where they had settled, fishing and navigation rights and the right to self-government and title after seven years. Meanwhile, their investors in England had secured vast tracts of land to dispose of however they saw fit whenever the opportunity presented itself. In many ways, the Second Pierce Patent was simply another "Particular Patent" like those issued to the colonists and investors by the Virginia Company under the First Pierce Patent, only now under the appropriate geographic jurisdiction. Clearly, Thomas Weston and John Pierce had secured the blessing of the Plymouth Council for their endeavor and carved a little slice of autonomy out for themselves in the region. Yet issues still remained. Boundaries were vague at best and appeared to be based on improvements (such as houses, farms, ports and fishing stages) as a manner of asserting claim over an area—and of course, the London Adventurers still expected a hefty return on their investment and would retain ownership if they chose not to sell their property to the colonists at the end of that time or if the colonists were unable to come up with the needed revenue.

In 1622, there began a flurry of activity to clarify patents and stake out claims over New England. This latest fevered round of legal and political wrangling in the back rooms and parlors of London and Plymouth, England, would result in the Virginia Company being placed in receivership in March 1622 and a completely new system for allotting property rights in New England. That year, the New England Company applied to and received approval from the King's Privy Council for a new allotment of territories in New England. This allotment carved up the territory into twenty roughly equal allotments beginning at the southernmost coast of what is now Rhode Island and ending near the mouth of the Bay of Fundy. The title for each allotment was given to one of twenty different influential nobles to dispose of and utilize as each saw fit. Sir Sam Argoll was granted lands around the Plymouth Colony, Lord Sheffield was granted the region around Cape Ann and then on up the coast; on paper at least, noble after noble now had claim and title over lands most had never been to and probably had no intention of ever visiting.[48] A few, such as Sir Fernando Gorges and the Earl of Arundel, who each laid claim to the northernmost parts of Maine, had some very specific ideas about fishing operations in the region. For most of the landholders though, these were merely viewed as having the profitable legal right to approve or disapprove of (and of course collect rents and profits from) the establishment of settlements, trading posts, plantations and fisheries in the region. In short, these were absentee landlords.

By drawing up the lands in allotments under specific nobles, the New England Company was able to establish at least some kind of legal method for using land that was familiar to Englishmen and had the effect of encouraging the development of and investment in several new companies interested in settling in and exploiting various resources in the region. One such company, the Dorchester Company (after the town in England where the investors were from), applied to Lord Sheffield for a fishing license to fish the waters off the coasts of his holdings in Cape Ann and to establish a fishing station and settlement there as well under the name of a member of the Dorchester Company named Richard Bushrod. Final approval for the project had to come from the Council on New England of course, but conveniently Lord Sheffield was also a member of that council and approval was not all that hard to obtain. By February 1623, everything was in order, and the council granted a patent to settle the area to yet another member of the Dorchester Company, Sir Walter Earle. A few months later, the Dorchester Company purchased and outfitted a ship, the *Fellowship*, to begin fishing in the area and exploring for a suitable site for a fishery and settlement.[49]

While the Dorchester Company was busy getting its ducks in a row for a new settlement and fishing post on Cape Ann, events at the Plymouth Colony were about to take a dramatic turn for the worse. In May 1622, the ship *Sparrow* arrived at the Plymouth Colony with a new batch of roughly sixty settlers employed by none other than Thomas Weston to establish yet another colony just north of Plymouth near present-day Weymouth, Massachusetts.[50] Thomas Weston was not with them but sent word that after he finished fishing for a season at Damariscove, Maine (near present-day Boothbay Harbor), that he would arrive with more supplies for the new colony. Also with the arrival of the *Sparrow* came a series of dispatches that showed that Thomas Weston had been thrown out of or resigned from the London Adventurers that had financed the Plymouth Colony. The London Adventurers had secreted a letter in the sole of a shoe of one of the colonists on the *Sparrow*—which had been discovered by Thomas Weston prior to embarking—and accused him of fraud and censoring communications between the London Adventurers and the Plymouth Colony. Weston had immediately included a retort to the accusations leveled against him in that letter and urged the Plymouth colonists not to place trust in the London Adventurers and treat the new settlers kindly. He also warned that the London Adventurers were seeking to abandon and cheat those of the Leyden Congregation still living in Holland and refusing to send supplies and provisions to the new colony.[51] To say that the leaders of the Plymouth

Colony were confused by these revelations and wary of both parties is a gross understatement. However, the fact remained that they now found themselves in the company of dozens of hungry new settlers cast with hardly any provisions upon their shores.

Known as the Wasagusquassett Colony, the Wessagusett Colony or Mr. Weston's Plantation at Wessagusett, this settlement would prove a thorn in the side of the Plymouth Colony, the local Natives and the later Massachusetts Colony for nearly a decade after its short-lived existence. The Wessagusett colonists had suffered much during their crossing, and many of them were sickly and ill-equipped for the hard labor required of establishing a new colony. At first, they were housed in the dwellings of the Plymouth colonists until they had recovered sufficiently to begin construction of the new settlement.[52] A short time after their arrival, a fishing vessel under one Captain Hudson arrived at the Plymouth Plantation with the shocking news of the massacre of colonists in Jamestown, Virginia, at the hands of the Powhatan people of that region.[53] After over a decade of encroachment, illness, exploitation and verbal and physical abuse, in May 1622, the Powhatan unleashed a sudden and devastating attack on the English colonists at Jamestown. Prior to the attack, the Powhatan entered several of the settlements around Jamestown peacefully and with various goods and foods to trade with the settlement. Once the Powhatan warriors were in position, some unknown signal was made, and the slaughter of the colonists began. In the attack, 347 men, women and children were killed outright, and the survivors retreated into several fortifications, where they were able to hold out against the Powhatan warriors.[54] Needless to say, as more and more of the details of the Jamestown Massacre became known, and then exaggerated, the level of anxiety at the northern colony increased dramatically. That the Native peoples of New England had no contact with the Powhatan of Virginia, were culturally as different from them as the English were from the Austrians and were experiencing completely different circumstances mattered little to the paranoid Plymouth colonists. Plymouth strengthened its fortifications and prepared for the worst.

Despite the fear gripping the hearts of the Plymouth colonists at this time, Thomas Weston's people soon set out to establish their new colony at Wessagusett. While the colonists paid little heed to the territorial claims of the Native peoples of the region, the site of the Wessagusett Colony was understood by both the Wampanoag (in whose territory the Plymouth Colony had been established) and the Massachusett to be clearly in the territory of the latter. This would mark the first time the Massachusett would have to deal with an English colony in their territory, and it would not be a positive experience.

In many ways, the Wessagusett colonists were set up to fail from the beginning. They were not well provisioned, and after the Plymouth Colony had sent a large portion of its food stores to aid the Jamestown Colony, their neighbors had little to spare for the new endeavor. Nor does it appear that the Plymouth colonists liked the Wessagusett colonists all that much. Plymouth Colony was not all that inclined to assist people employed by Thomas Weston, whose reputation had justifiably fallen quite low over the past two years. With little food, supplies or trade goods and completely ignorant of even the most basic means of survival in the New World, the Wessagusett colonists would soon strain the already fragile relationship between the Massachusett and the Plymouth Colony.

To be fair to both the Plymouth colonists and the Massachusett, neither were expecting the arrival of the Wessagusett colonists and neither had extensive food stores to spare. The Massachusett, like the rest of the Native peoples of southern New England, never horded that much of a surplus of their summer corn crop, keeping only enough to supplement their winter diet of shellfish, ground nuts, wild fowl and other game. The Plymouth colonists had little enough to spare either. The winter of 1620–21 had been extremely trying for the Plymouth Colony, and over half their number died from starvation, malnutrition, exposure and associated illnesses. The summer of 1621 and the subsequent winter of 1621–22 had been much easier for the Plymouth Colony, and the settlers had learned quite a bit about how to plant crops, gather shellfish and hunt wild game; what to expect from the change of seasons; and how to plan accordingly. However, a severe drought had struck the region in the summer of 1622, and the yield from the corn crop that year suffered as a result. After assisting the Jamestown Colony with what little surplus they had, there was just barely enough to see themselves through the winter, let alone some sixty additional mouths to feed.

By February 1623, the overseer of the Wessagusett Colony, John Sanders, was begging the Plymouth Colony and the Massachusett for food. Neither party offered any assistance, so Sanders requested permission from the Plymouth Colony to take provisions from the Massachusett by force. This too was denied, and soon the Wessagusett colonists began stealing food from the Massachusett. When the Massachusett confronted the Wessagusett colonists about the thefts, the colonists laid the blame on one of their own number who was a "poor, decrepit old man, that was unserviceable to the company, and burthensome to keep alive,"[55] and had him hanged.

Inevitably, as the situation of the Wessagusett colonists became more and more desperate, thieving from the Massachusett continued. William Bradford later recalled:

> *And after they began to come into wants, many sold away their clothes and bed coverings; others (so base were they) became servants to the Indians, and would cut them wood and fetch them water for a capful of corn; others fell into plain stealing, both night and day, from the Indians, of which they grievously complained. In the end, they came to that misery that some starved and died with cold and hunger. One in gathering shellfish was so weak as he stuck fast in the mud and was found dead in that place. At last most of them left their dwellings and scattered up and down the woods and by the watersides, where they could find ground nuts and clams, here six and there ten.*[56]

Around this time, word reached the Plymouth colonists that their ally and friend, the Sachem Massasoit of the Wampanoag, was grievously ill, and they sent a small party to visit him and render what assistance they could. There, Massasoit informed the Plymouth colonists that he had been approached by the Massachusett to either join with them on an attack on both colonies or to stand by while the Massachusett attacked on their own. It seems that the Massachusett had had enough of the diseased and thieving Wessagusett colonists but feared that if they attacked them that Plymouth would retaliate. They had decided that the only safe course of action was to exterminate both colonies in one devastating blow. Massasoit had opposed this move by the Massachusett, but given his poor state of health, he could physically do little about it.

On March 24, 1623, Massasoit's warnings were proven true when one of the Wessagusett colonists, thirty-two-year-old Phineas Pratt, arrived at Plymouth in a desperate state and claiming that the Massachusett were on the verge of attacking both settlements. The next day, Plymouth dispatched a small force under Myles Standish to inflict a preemptive strike on the Massachusett and extricate whatever Wessagusett colonists still survived.[57] Accompanying Standish's party was a Wampanoag named Hobbamock. Phineas Pratt, being too weak to travel, stayed behind.

When Standish and his party reached the site of the Wessagusett Colony, he found that colony's one remaining ship left completely unguarded and empty, while the other ship had set out under John Sanders to attempt to secure food from English fishermen at Monhegan Island, Maine. Upon discharging a musket, the captain and the remainder of the crew came in from the shore, where they had been scrounging for ground nuts and clams. Standish ordered that all the Wessagusett colonists should return to the town (as they had spread themselves out, each in a desperate search for food) and issued each present a pint of corn taken from Plymouth's precious supply of seed.

The next few days proved stormy, and Standish's men and the surviving Wessagusett colonists sheltered in the crude huts erected there. Soon a Massachusett man approached them, ostensibly to trade furs; Standish suspected him of being a spy. After the Massachusett man left, more Massachusett gradually arrived. One named Pecksuot approached Hobbamock and inquired if Standish intended to kill the Massachusett at Wessagusett, to which Hobbamock responded vaguely. Another among the Massachusett visitors was a warrior named Wituwamat, who brought with him a knife with a woman's face carved into the handle. Wituwamat took a seat across from Standish and began sharpening the blade. Wituwamat then told of how he had another knife, much like this one, only with a man's face, and that he had killed both French and Englishmen with that blade; he then made a menacing joke that soon the two blades must marry before retiring for the night. The next day, Wituwamat returned to the hut with a small party of Massachusett. Upon their entrance, Standish gave a signal to his men outside to bar the door and then snatched Wituwamat's knife from him and stabbed him in the neck with it. The rest of his men fell upon the Massachusett and slaughtered them. Hobbamock stood by and watched, saying afterward to Standish, "Though you are a great Captain, yet you are but a little man. But today I see you are big enough to lay him on the ground."[58] Soon after, the English fell upon the Massachusett throughout the town, killing all but one, who managed to escape and raise the alarm. Standish gathered up his party, the surviving Wessagusett colonists, a few Massachusett women they had captured and the severed head of Wituwamat and began the retreat back to Plymouth. After a brief skirmish on the way with a band of Massachusett, they arrived at Plymouth safely, where the captive Massachusett women were freed. Standish impaled the head of Wituwamat on a pike above the gate of the fort as a clear message to the Massachusett and any other Native peoples that might wish harm on the English.[59]

The remaining Wessagusett colonists were given the choice of remaining in Plymouth, under the laws and commands of the leadership of that colony, or setting out on their own. A few, including Phineas Pratt, elected

Myles Standish assaults Wituwamat at Wessagussett in this 1878 print. *Courtesy of the New York Public Library.*

to stay. However, the vast majority had had enough of this New England and elected to return home to old England and so soon departed for Monhegan Island and Damariscove, Maine, in the hopes of finding work on a fishing vessel that made seasonal voyages from the coast there back to England.

Thomas Weston soon arrived in Plymouth for the first time after a harrowing voyage from Damariscove, which found him shipwrecked in Ipswich Bay, then robbed of everything save for literally the shirt off his back by the Massachusett in the area. He escaped to the fishing station at Pascataqua (now Portsmouth, New Hampshire) and eventually was able to find passage on another fishing vessel to Plymouth in high hopes that he would find the foundation laid for a flourishing colony at Wessagusett. Needless to say, he was rather disappointed. Yet, likely for lack of any other options, he chose to remain at Plymouth.[60]

While the relationship between the Plymouth colonists and the Massachusett was considerably soured as a result of the Wessagusett Colony, tensions appear to have simmered down a bit once that colony had ceased to exist and both the Massachusett and the Plymouth colonists began to busy themselves with the spring planting—or so it would seem. Decades later, in 1662, Phineas Pratt, who was at that time the last surviving participant in the Wessagusett disaster, wrote an account of that year, revealing further conflicts between the Massachusett and the Plymouth colonists. Most of what we know about the Plymouth and later Massachusetts colonies in the early years of the colonies come from the writings of William Bradford (former governor and self-appointed historian of the Plymouth Colony), William Hubbard (a priest who settled in Ipswich after 1630, became friends with many original settlers and wrote a history of the Massachusetts Colony) and an essay incredibly critical of the Plymouth Colony written by Thomas Morton in the 1640s. Each of these sources, and most especially Bradford's, while chronologically correct, were written by men who were much more concerned with preserving their own legacies than preserving a history. For example, William Bradford never once mentions Roger Conant by name, and Thomas Morton mostly wrote about how horrible William Bradford and his contemporaries were to "strangers" and Native peoples alike. Thus each must be taken with a grain of salt. Yet none of them mention anything about the events that Phineas Pratt recorded, and perhaps there was a reason why Pratt would wait until all those who could contradict him were dead.

In his account, Phineas Pratt recalled that two Englishmen (who were not mentioned by William Bradford) had been captured during the fighting at Wessagusett and later tortured to death. Shortly after, Pratt was on a ship that seized a canoe manned by a Massachusett warrior named Abordikees. Pratt's account is as follows:

> *Two of Abordikees men came tither, and seeing me said, "When we killed your men, they cried and made ill-favored faces." I said, "When we killed your men, we did not torment them to make ourselves merry." Then we went with our ship into the bay and took from them two shallops loading of corn, and of their men, prisoners. There is a town of later time called Dorchester. The third and last time was in the bay of Agawam. At this time they took for their castle a thick swamp. At this time one of our ablest men was shot in the shoulder. Whether any of them were killed or wounded we could not tell. There is a town of later time near unto the place, called Ipswich.*[61]

If Phineas Pratt's account is to be believed, then fighting between the Plymouth colonists and the Massachusett lasted into the summer of 1623 and was far more brutal and costly to both the Plymouth Colony and the

RETURN OF MILES STANDISH FROM WESSAGUSSET.

Return of Myles Standish from Wessagussett with Wituwamat's head on a pike. *Courtesy of the New York Public Library.*

Massachusett than is stated in either Bradford or Hubbard's accounts. Both Dorchester and Agawam (Ipswich) lay deep in the heart of Massachusett territory, much farther than the border areas of Wessagusett.

Despite of all of the unknowns, schemes, half-truths, property disputes, conflicting patents, accusations and counter accusations that swirled around the events and people of southern New England in the year of 1623, one fact does become abundantly clear: this New World was a world of conflict. This was a world of abundant natural resources that existed alongside massive starvation and famine. This was a world where Englishmen warily eyed other Englishmen while living in constant fear and mistrust of the Native peoples whose lands they had come to inhabit and exploit. Likewise, this was a land where Native peoples warily eyed other Native peoples and struggled to figure out how to best use these new Englishmen in their never-ending feuds with one another—or whether to just get rid of them.

It was into this crazy new world of conflicting loyalties and motivations that a young salter of East Budleigh, England, named Roger Conant was about to step foot in along with his soon-to-be pregnant wife and infant son to start a new life in a new world. It is perhaps fitting then that among the first sights the young family would have seen on stepping off the ship at Plymouth was the head of a Native Massachusett warrior mounted on a pike.

ROGER CONANT AND THE SALT TRADE OF SEVENTEENTH-CENTURY LONDON

S o much of Roger Conant's life up until his settlement at Cape Ann remains a mystery, and it is likely for this reason more than any other that he has been largely ignored by biographers and historians of the early settlement of Massachusetts. Records of his time in England prior to emigrating are few and scattered. He seems to have been almost consciously left out of the history of the region written by William Bradford (who only makes mention dismissively of a "salter"). William Hubbard, who knew Roger Conant fairly intimately, does provide a great deal of insight into his life and activities in between 1624 and 1629 in his *History of New England*, but nothing is mentioned of Conant's early life prior to his arrival in North America.

Roger Conant was baptized in the church of East Budleigh, Devonshire, on April 9, 1592, and was the youngest of eight children. His father, Richard Conant, was a churchwarden from the class of landowners that owned some substantial property yet had no title of nobility—known at the time as the "middling sort." Roger's maternal grandfather, a man whose last name was Clarke, seized on the opportunity to purchase from the Crown a substantial portion of the former holdings of Sir Henry Courtenay, First Earl of Devon, after that noble was beheaded for treason by Henry VIII in 1538.[62] When the Crown found itself short on cash a few years later, it sold off large portions of Courtenay's former estates and thus provided Roger Conant's grandfather the rare opportunity in Tudor England to become a substantial landowner himself. The property that Grandfather Clarke

Birthplace of Sir Walter Raleigh, Budleigh, England. *Courtesy of the New York Public Library.*

purchased abutted the property on which the famous soldier, explorer and New World adventurer Sir Walter Raleigh was born in 1552. While there is no evidence that Raleigh ever returned to East Budleigh during Roger Conant's childhood or adolescence, it is safe to assume that Conant's parents knew Raleigh at least to some degree and that young Roger probably grew up following the exploits of the local town hero rather closely.

During the late sixteenth and early seventeenth centuries, East Budleigh was, like much of the rest of the West Country, a fishing community. For more than a century prior to Roger's birth, fishermen from East Budleigh and other parts of Devonshire had been making extended voyages far out into the North Atlantic in search of cod, and thus West Country men enjoyed a fair amount of functional knowledge of the coast of northeastern North America, far more than their compatriots in the rest of England.

The West Country was also a land of more traditional religious leanings then much of the rest of England during this time. While it is true that later in life Roger Conant became an active member of the Puritan First Church of Salem and helped establish First Parish in Beverly, Massachusetts, there is nothing about his early life to indicate that he harbored any extreme religious viewpoints. Indeed, if either he or his family had then that would have been at such odds with the prevailing West Country sentiments of that time that it is likely that there would have been some notice or mention made of it. While far from being devout Catholics, West Country Englishmen, like maritime peoples the world over, were far more superstitious and traditional in their religious leanings than either the Puritans or the Pilgrims would have been comfortable with. West Country people valued their traditions. They erected maypoles to celebrate May Day festivities (a practice quickly banned by the Pilgrims in Plymouth Plantation), placed horseshoes over their doors to ward off evil spirits and greatly feared the wrath of the fairies that inhabited the ancient Neolithic sites that dotted their homeland. West Countrymen made little fuss when the Church of England under Henry VIII broke away from the Roman Catholic Church, despite the fact that they relished the old Catholic feast days for the saints, the Latin prayers and the rituals of transubstantiation. So long as they could enjoy practicing their religious beliefs as their fathers, grandfathers and great-grandfathers had, they cared little about any disputes between their sovereign and the pope. However, when Protestant reforms affecting the manner in which they worshipped were forcefully introduced, they could react with extreme violence, as they did during the Prayer Book Rebellion in 1549.

Events later in Roger Conant's life also allude to more moderate religious leanings. Sometime in the early 1630s, Roger Conant sent his eldest son, Caleb, back to England to be educated under the tutelage of his older brother John Conant, a minister in the Church of England. Sadly, Caleb Conant died of some illness there in 1633.[63] It must be noted that the 1630s were a time when the more radical-leaning Puritan reformers had fallen out of favor with the Crown. The slightly Protestant-tolerant James I had passed away in 1625, and Charles I now sat on the throne. Charles I was vehemently opposed to the Puritans and favored a more traditional Church of England with all the pomp and circumstance that, just like the maypole to the Puritan mind, smacked of idolatry. Charles I's crackdown on Puritans in the late 1620s and early 1630s sent scores fleeing from his oppressive reign to the shores of New England and, in a few years, led to open civil war in England. If Roger Conant had been a fervent Puritan, it would be odd indeed for him to send his eldest son to be educated by the Church of England at the height of this unrest. Despite Roger Conant's later involvement with the Puritan churches in Salem and Beverly, it would be presumptuous to assume that this indicates that he was a Puritan. After all, these were the only churches in the area at the time. Much of the early records of these churches have been lost, but what has been preserved hardly paints Roger Conant as an ardent Puritan. For example, in 1659, when Roger Conant headed the petition to establish a church at Beverly, he wrote,

> *Wee your petitioners, (beeing upwards of Sixty families, who by reason of our inconveniency of meeting publiquely upon the Lords dayes at Salem Towne, it beeing very troublesome and dangerous, to transport ourselves and families winter and sommer over the ferry)…crave and request…that Your Worships would be pleased…that we may be a township or villedg of & by ourselves.…These things we leave to your wise consideration, hopeing that your bowells will move toward us in granteing your poor petitioners requests.*[64]

Unlike other divisions within towns and churches in New England during the seventeenth century, this division was about convenience rather than ideology or dogma. Beverly lay across the river from Salem, and it was difficult and often dangerous to cross during rough weather (a fact that any resident of either city would be sympathetic with even today). In order to establish a new town, there had to, by law, be a new church established. It is in this and other similar capacities that we see the work of Roger Conant when it comes to his involvement in the church. In fact, what becomes glaringly obvious is his complete absence from the various religious controversies that would engulf these churches during his later years, as various First Churches across New England—and especially in Salem and Beverly—split into different congregations as a result of arguments over dogma and governance.

It is difficult to prescribe with any certainty all that much about Roger Conant's religious leanings or upbringing. What does mark him as rather exceptional is that he appeared to (with only a few notable exceptions) have a unique ability to get along well with many different people with different viewpoints and that he viewed the church as an integral part of any community. In this he was probably not all that dissimilar with most working people of any cosmopolitan trade at any time in human history. In any trade that requires interaction with people from multiple different backgrounds, one has to be flexible—and Roger Conant was certainly about to embark on such a career when he left East Budleigh at the tender age of eighteen.

In 1611, Roger Conant arrived in London to join his older brother Christopher, who had left East Budleigh in 1609 to become a grocer in that massive metropolis. Both brothers appear to have done fairly well for themselves. By 1616, Christopher was admitted to the Grocers Company and shortly thereafter married a woman named Anne Wilton and set up

The 1633 seal of the Salters
Company of London. *Courtesy of the
University of Victoria.*

a shop in St. Lawrence, Jewry. By 1618, Roger had joined the Salters Company, married a woman named Sarah Horton and settled in his brother's neighborhood.[65]

Joining the Salters Company (or as it is officially known, the Master, Wardens and Commonality of the Art or Mystery of the Salters of London) and identifying as a salter does not necessarily mean that Roger Conant became a skilled maker of salt. Given the lack of salt production in England during his lifetime it is far more likely that Roger Conant was a skilled craftsman with expertise is using salt for food preservation, as someone who set the measurement standards for a market known as a "salt meter" or someone with some other skill related to the salt trade. It did mean, though, that Roger Conant was joining one of the few organizations that provided an outlet for working-class tradesmen to have influence in both civil government and the British economy in seventeenth-century England. While much of the records of the Salters Company were lost in the Great London Fire of 1666, it is fairly obvious that being a member of the company would play a major role in Roger Conant's life and the events that led him to immigrate to the New World to assist with the establishment of fisheries. Eventually, he became governor of a fledging colony on the coast of what would become Salem, Massachusetts. Given the importance the organization played in his life, economics, craft, connections and motivations, it is important for us to understand where the Salters Company came from and the role it played in the working-class politics of English society during Roger Conant's lifetime.

Along with the rest of the livery companies and guilds of London, the Salters Company dated to the fourteenth century when craftsmen began to organize to improve their conditions and economic clout in a manner similar to trade unions today. Twenty members of the Salters Company have served as Lord Mayor of London. Thomas Walpole, the ancestor of Prime Minister Robert Walpole and MP Thomas Walpole, began his family's long and intergenerational relationship with English politics as a salter in the fourteenth century.[66] By the 1300s, Bread Street had become the center of the salt trade in London (it remained the center of the salt trade when the Conant brothers would settle near there two hundred years later), and soon the company began to elect its members to the Court of

Common Council in order to further the interests of their craft. By 1394, this predecessor of the Salters Company was considered such a stabilizing force in London's economy that Richard II officially recognized it by issuing a royal license to found the Fraternity and Guild of Corpus Christi in the Church of All Hallows, Bread Street. This fraternity set standards on quality, pricing, weights and measures and had the authority to impose financial penalties on violators. It also set up apprentices for specific trades, performed charitable work for its less fortunate members and often provided a path for its members toward political influence in ways that were often unattainable for commoners in England during this time.

For much of English history, salt was an imported necessity, especially in London. For most of the Middle Ages in Europe, salt was harvested from one of three primary sources: directly from mining rock salt from salt mines (as was common in Germany and parts of Spain), allowing seawater to evaporate in shallow man-made pools and then collecting the salt crystals left over or burning peat from salt marshes. There was quite a great deal of variation in techniques to harvest salt from any of these sources throughout Europe, but unfortunately for the English, geography cursed the British Isles with few resources to harvest salt locally. Rock salt mines are conspicuously absent throughout the islands, and the cloudy and moist climate does not lend itself well to evaporation. Peat moss salt was harvested throughout England, but that was considered a low-quality salt (it was known as "grey salt" because it was grey and ashy) and was not all that much trusted as a food preservative— perhaps peat ash just doesn't lend itself well to flavor. There was also a common perception at the time that seafood had to be preserved in sea salt, and as the English fishing fleet was exploding on the European market beginning in the Middle Ages, the demand for sea salt grew with it. Some English sea salt was manufactured through evaporation in Droitwich and Cheshire, but most of these English sites were not able to keep up with the huge demand for salt and were considered low quality. The salt that was used for preserving English fish was mostly imported from the Biscay coast of France.[67] As a result, most members of the Salters Company were employed in the importation, packing and packaging of salt rather than its manufacture, although there undoubtedly a few salters who were familiar with the production of salt itself. Upon arriving at Billingsgate in London, a salt meter would, with the help of a servant, measure the salt into barrels so that a common unit of measurement could be enjoyed by all who engaged in the salt trade in London. After the salt was metered out, salt porters would then carry the salt to different markets (mostly located near Bread Street).[68]

One of the first victories for the Salters Company and its elected representatives on the Common Council was to gain a degree of control over the appointment salt meters. At first, the Salters Company actively campaigned for the direct election of salt meters by the general population, but this campaign led to the company being fined in 1419 by the Lord Mayor of London for having "usurped the state of the City."[69] Obviously, the powers of London at that time were not all that comfortable with the city's recent foray into democracy under the 1384 Charter revision. The Salters Company dutifully paid the fine but didn't give up on the campaign. Instead, the members changed their strategy and engaged in what today would be considered a massive public relations campaign: they purchased large quantities of salt to distribute for "the Common Good of the Citizens of London."[70] These efforts soon paid off, and eventually public pressure forced the city to enter into a compromise with the Salters Company. While the City of London would still retain the right to appoint salt meters, it could choose only candidates who were nominated by the Salters Company—including members of the Salters Company itself.

Over the course of the fifteenth and sixteenth centuries, the City of London and the Crown began to rely more and more heavily on the various guilds—and particularly the Salters Company—as not only a stabilizing force for the region's economy but also a source of needed revenue and manpower during trying times. The Salters Company loaned money to the city and the Crown on several occasions, most notably during the reign of Elizabeth I, when it not only provided large sums for outfitting ships against the Spanish Armada but also outfitted and raised a company of 160 salters for the defense of Blackheath. In 1596, the Salters Company outfitted and manned fourteen vessels for the English attack on Cadiz, Spain. By the beginning of the seventeenth century, the Salters Company, had begun to maintain an armory at its guild hall in order to outfit members in case the city of London came under attack. Despite these forays into military service, the most vital work the various guilds provided to the city during this time came in the forms of loans and food. London was rapidly growing, and by the end of the seventeenth century, it would be home to well over 2 million inhabitants. Feeding such a large population is a difficult task even in modern times, but in that era, a single bad harvest could mean famine and devastation. In 1521, 1545 and 1630, the guilds agreed to use a portion of their members' dues for the purchase of food for the general population of the city.[71]

In spite of the growing role the Salters Company played in civic service, its primary purpose remained the economic empowerment of its members.

In the 1630s, Charles I attempted to establish a royal monopoly on the salt trade in England. By 1630, religious conflict in France had curtailed trade from La Rochelle, which happened to be the main port from which French salt was imported to England and resulted in a bit of a salt shortage in the country. Charles I decided to seize on this opportunity to ramp up domestic Scottish, English and Irish salt production while simultaneously creating a royal monopoly over salt in which the Crown would set the price of salt and sell licenses to Crown favorites while taking a cut of each barrel of salt collected by the salt meters: £4 per barrel for domestic use with 10s being paid to the Crown or £3 10s for use in the fisheries, with the Crown taking 3s 4d out of every barrel. The Salters Company did not believe that ramping up domestic salt production was all that realistic given the geographic difficulties in producing local high-quality salt and felt that the Crown's real aim was simply to increase its own revenue. What the salters most feared was the establishment of a royal monopoly over the production and importation of salt governed by royal appointees over whom they could have little, if any, influence. At first, the Salters Company offered "to pay what imposition, voluntary on salt, the king may please to lay"[72] if Charles I would simply forgo establishing a monopoly. The king refused and, in 1635, established the Society of Salters, a royal monopoly governed by royal appointees that was to have complete oversight and control over all domestic salt production and foreign salt importation.[73]

Petitions against the royal monopoly predictably failed to garner any consideration from Charles I, and by 1638, the Salters Company had begun to change their tactics. The company formed an alliance with the Fishmongers Guild (whose membership was employed in the packaging and trading of preserved fish and whose trade was obviously wholly dependent on a ready supply of cheap, high-quality salt) and reached out to the communities of Southampton, Rye, Sandwich and Dover (all vital towns to the importation and distribution of salt in England) to set up what today would be called organizing committees to coordinate opposition to the king's monopoly. The Fishmongers Guild and the Salters Company then hired a Mr. Hearne to serve as their legal counsel. The coalition met in the Mermaid Tavern on Bread Street in London to draw up one final petition to the King's Privy Council in opposition to the monopoly, and predictably, once again the Privy Council rejected the petition. Salters and fishmongers began protesting in the streets of London while their allies in Southampton, Rye, Sandwich and Dover began a systematic campaign of refusing to cooperate with monopoly officials in those cities. The economic impact of these coordinated actions on the Society of Salters was devastating. By 1640, Mr. Hoarth, a leading member of the Society of Salters and a Crown favorite, was heavily in debt, owing £13,500 to the Crown and an additional £4,500 to shareholders who had invested in the crown monopoly. While pleading for leniency from the debtors' courts, Hoarth railed against "a combination of trade, if any used, by the London Salters."[74] The monopoly had become a complete failure, and without the cooperation of the guilds and the allied cities, any control on paper from the Crown became impossible to enforce. The Society of Salters remained a paper Crown monopoly throughout the short-lived reign of Charles I—after which it was finally disbanded by Cromwell—until the Lord Protector seized power following the English Civil War, yet it was so powerless that it might as well have ceased to exist. The Salters Company and its allies had taken on the king of England and won.

While Roger Conant had long since moved to New England by the time of the campaign against Charles I, those who participated in that campaign were of the same generation of salters as Roger Conant, and many of the leaders in that movement would have been his contemporaries. When Roger Conant joined the Salters Company in 1618, he wasn't simply entering into an apprenticeship program or some exclusive men's club, he was joining a well-established and structured labor guild whose membership was extremely active in the political and economic struggles of seventeenth-century England. This was an organization that not only trained its membership in the skills needed to perform their craft and set standards by which the industry governed itself but also actively encouraged and promoted its membership in both civic engagement and political power with real, tangible results. At this time, the Salters Company was also a strict organization with a clear hierarchy of elected members, called wardens, who formed the governing body of the organization. Upon being accepted into the guild, Roger Conant would have taken the following oath:

> *To be loyal to the Sovereign, to keep the peace of the City, to preserve the secrets of the Fellowship, to prevent any designs against it and inform the Wardens thereupon, to obey the ordinances of the Craft, to come when summoned by its Wardens or else pay a fine (unless good reason existed for absence), to contribute to the Craft's charges, to bring any complaints against others of the Fellowship before the Wardens before carrying such disputes elsewhere; to serve any office to which they might be chosen, and generally behave well and truly for the weal and warship of the Craft.*[75]

This oath was made before God and in the church on Bread Street and was thus enforceable by church law rather than civil law. Oaths were a serious matter during this time, and the Church of England maintained courts presided over by clergy to determine whether or not an oath taker had broken their oath and had the right to impose fines, penalties and even excommunication for those the church found guilty. Yet the church had only the authority to determine whether or not the oath itself had been violated. By swearing an oath to "bring all complaints against others of the Fellowship before the Wardens," members of the Salters Company were able to set up a system by which all disputes that erupted in their trade could be handled internally. Likewise, through the election of the wardens, the common membership was able to exercise some degree of control and ownership over the manner in which the rules of their trade were governed and implemented. This constitutes a dramatic step forward toward the idea of self-government, and it should come as no surprise that the first instance in which we see common people actively practicing this concept in modern England (and by extension modern America) would be in their work lives. After all, decisions made about someone's livelihood will have more of a direct and immediate effect on that individual's well-being than nearly any other facet of social, civic or religious life. In addition to using the oath to set up a structure by which disputes could be resolved internally, by insisting that members of the Salters Company swear to "preserve the secrets of the Fellowship" and to "obey the Ordinances of the Craft," the Salters Company was ensuring that those skilled jobs that required expertise remained fully under the control of the guild. This solidified the guild's control over the industry as a whole by restricting the necessary training for such trade crafts to those who would be members.

This isn't to say that the Salters Company wasn't at times in its own history somewhat tyrannical in certain aspects of its members' lives. Despite the organization's democratic structure and focus on improving the economic and social standing of its membership, it at times dabbled a little into what might be considered totalitarianism. Around the end of the sixteenth and beginning of the seventeenth centuries (roughly the same period that Roger Conant joined the Salters Company), the Salters Company began to become a bit obsessed with its members' private lives. In defense of the company, much of its economic and political clout at this time depended in large part on the positive perception it enjoyed from the general public after the organization's relief efforts following the various near famines of the sixteenth century and willingness to arm its membership and defend England against the hated papist Spanish. Thus it is at least somewhat understandable that the wardens of the Salters Company would be concerned with how their membership governed themselves in public, yet such concern is often a slippery slope that can lead to either ridiculousness or outright oppression. This is made evident by an edict passed by the wardens of the Salters Company in the closing years of the sixteenth century. Among more mundane matters regarding the governing of young salter apprentices, it read that members should not

> *suffer their apprentices to swear or blaspheme the name of God, to haunt evil women, schools of fence or dancing, carding, bowling, tennis play or other unlawful games, to resort to taverns or alehouses (except about their master's business) to wear any ruffs on their shirts, nor in hosen any other color than white, russet, watchet, or blue, and to be made plain without any welts, guards, or cuts, and to have no manner of silk in or upon their hosen. The apprentice who obstinately offends to be scourged in our Hall.*[76]

How much of this could have been enforced remains to be seen, and it clearly applied only to apprentices and not to fully established members of the guild. Still, it is quite clear that the leadership of the Salters Company was becoming quite concerned about raising up the "right sort" of future membership and was more than willing to wade into the personal lives of their apprentices to ensure the right kind of upbringing. At any rate, these rules were in effect during Roger Conant's apprenticeship with the Salters Company and would have applied to him.

At first, the Salters Company restricted its membership to those who worked in either the manufacture, marketing or use of salt. However, given that salt was the most widespread and effective method of food preservation at this time, it was inevitable that all manner of crafts would in some way work directly with salt. Anything that required a long voyage required some kind of functional knowledge about salt, and before long, the Salters Company opened its ranks to nearly anyone in any craft so long as they paid their dues and adhered to the organization's standard of conduct.[77]

That the Salters Company was one of the few livery companies with an open membership has caused some, such as Roger Conant's biographer Clifford Shipton, to question whether Conant ever really was a salter by trade or simply some kind of businessman who happened to be a member of the organization. Given that the Conant brothers settled so close to Bread Street, the dire need for experienced salters in the fishing outposts of New England, the manner in which he was always referred to as a salter and the fact that salt remained the primary focus of the Salters Company no matter how much it may have changed over the centuries, it seems perfectly reasonable to assume that Roger Conant was indeed a salter by trade in at least some capacity. The evidence that Roger Conant was a member of the company comes from his membership in the Salters' Parish Church and the references to him by his contemporaries, but not from the Salters Company itself. In 1607, the company received a royal charter and its present name from James I. All records from that date on were housed in a new facility, which then burned to the ground in the London Fire of 1666.[78]

In addition to Roger Conant's involvement with the Salters Company, there are a few other insights into the Conant family's life in London during the years leading up to their immigration to the New World. Both Roger and Christopher were living in London on that fateful October day in 1618 when Walter Raleigh was beheaded for treason. Of all the royal executions in the history of England, the execution of a national hero of such stature as Walter Raleigh just to pacify the hated Spanish was arguably one of the least popular. Raleigh, after all, was the hero who defeated the Spanish Armada, who thumbed his nose at the powerful Spanish navy in engagement after engagement and who introduced the joys of tobacco to all of England. More than a hero, he was a celebrity, especially to those Protestant-minded Englishmen who read of his exploits against the papist Spanish with glee.

Walter Raleigh had been previously imprisoned for nearly thirteen years in the Tower of London for treason after his conviction of involvement in a plot to replace King James I. Many felt that the charges against him were unfounded, and the king chose to commute his death sentence and instead imprison him the Tower of London. Nearly immediately after Raleigh's release, the Spanish ambassador discovered that Raleigh was outfitting twelve vessels for some kind of expedition. He alerted the Spanish court in Madrid that Raleigh was likely preparing for an invasion of Guinea, a region of South America that Spain had recently settled but that Walter Raleigh had laid claim to for the English Crown twenty-three years earlier. Raleigh readily admitted that Guinea was his destination, but he assured both King James I and the Spanish ambassador that he was outfitting an expedition to discover a gold mine he had been told of during his previous exploration of the region. King James I gave the expedition his tacit blessing, and the Spanish began fortifying the region. When Raleigh's expedition arrived at the Orinoco River, he proceeded to blockade and sack the Spanish town of Santo Tome de Guyana. Upon his return to England in 1618, the Spanish were furious and demanded that King

SIR WALTER RALEIGH
beheaded in Old Palace Yard.

Execution of Sir Walter
Raleigh in London,
England, 1618. *Courtesy of
the New York Public Library.*

James I execute Raleigh for violating the peace with Spain. King James
I promptly condemned Walter Raleigh to death. Raleigh's execution, like
nearly all executions during that time, was public, and it is likely that the
Conant brothers were present for it. For the young Conant brothers, who
grew up next door to Raleigh's childhood home, the execution of their
boyhood hometown hero was likely hard to witness.

On September 19, 1619, Roger and Sarah Conant brought their firstborn
daughter to Saint Lawrence Parish to be christened and named the baby after
her mother. Less than thirteen months later, Roger and Sarah returned to the
parish to bury the infant Sarah. Three years later, in 1622, Roger and Sarah
returned to the parish for the christening of their next child, Caleb Conant,
who would live to see adulthood.[79] While infant mortality was not all that

uncommon during this period in any part of the world, especially England, life was hard for the young Conant family in London during the first few years of the 1620s. This was a time of massive economic, religious and social change in England, as the island nation was just beginning to emerge into the modern era as a major world power. Trade, especially foreign trade, was becoming more and more essential to the economy of England. Pastoralism was slowly giving way toward an early form of industrialization. Cities exploded in population as the country peasants flocked to them for what little work they could find. Meanwhile, the Crown sought to manipulate this new emerging economy by granting licenses and trade monopolies to court favorites. To say that this had a disastrous effect on the population would be a gross overstatement. England would, after all, emerge from this period as the dominant world power, arguably even the first real superpower of the modern age. Yet changing times are stressful times, especially for working people, as old patterns of subsistence give way to new ones. The Reverend John White of Dorchester (a contemporary of Roger Conant) summed up the plight of working people in England during this time: "Many among us live without employment, either wholly, or in the greatest part…and that doe not onely such as delight in idleness; but even folke willing to labour, who live without exercise in their callings."[80]

While England was going through this period of intense economic, social and political change and Englishmen were likewise going through a period of great economic uncertainty, it was becoming more and more apparent that there was a great unfulfilled need to establish a productive saltworks somewhere in the vicinity of New England. The booming English cod industry required massive amounts of salt that, as has been previously discussed, were not available domestically to the English. More importantly, cod had to be salted on-site, and this meant that English fishermen had to import their salt first to England and then ship it with them across the Atlantic on their fishing voyages. How much cod they could catch was entirely dependent on the amount of salt they brought with them. If they caught more fish than they had salt for, the excess fish would simply be a waste. The English had set up some saltworks illegally on Spanish possessions in the Caribbean, where they made sea salt through evaporation. English sailors would winter over on these various islands (such as Salt Cay in the Turks and Caicos) and spend the winter making salt before shipping off to Nova Scotia, Newfoundland or New England (regions where the lack of heat and sunlight made making salt by evaporation difficult), but this was a tenuous solution at best to the problem. In the sixteenth and early seventeenth centuries, the

Caribbean was nearly entirely dominated by the Spanish, and the Spanish and the English were constantly at odds. Warfare between the two nations was frequent, and the Spanish had a much larger naval presence in the area. Relying solely on imported salt meant that the English fishing industry was under a constant threat from rival foreign powers.

It was also well known that Massachusetts Bay lined up at roughly the same latitude as the Bay of Biscay, which was one of the primary sources of producing sea salt via evaporation in Europe. Indeed, the vast majority of the sea salt consumed in England at this time was imported from that region. To the seventeenth-century mind—completely ignorant of the impact of the earth's tilt, currents and trade winds on climate (the Gulf Stream would not be "discovered" until the eighteenth century) and by and large still fairly unaware of the physical geography of North America—it seemed entirely logical that Massachusetts Bay should be able to produce just as much high-quality sea salt as the Bay of Biscay if they could just establish a large saltworks in the region. Or, at least, that's how it seemed to the men in the drawing rooms and coffeehouses of London poring over maps of the region. Unfortunately for the English, while they had many experts in the use of salt for preserving food, there were few Englishmen who knew how to actually produce high-quality sea salt through evaporation. Although, given that salt was such a common commodity, a general understanding of the process was quite common. The preferred method of making sea salt at this time was through evaporation. This was a relatively simple process in which seawater was pumped or poured into vats lined with clay and left exposed to the sun. After the water had evaporated, salt workers then scraped the salt out of the vats. However, this process required a great deal of sunlight (something that New England is not necessarily known for) and required about four hundred gallons of seawater to make one bushel of salt. Salt could also be produced by simply boiling seawater, but this required a great deal of fuel. The only fuel source available to the colonists at this time and place was from trees and thus was an extremely costly endeavor. Early New Englanders kept a kettle of seawater simmering over their fireplaces all day to make salt for personal use, but this would never produce the quantity needed to sustain a large fishing operation. Even if establishing a functioning saltworks on par with those of the Bay of Biscay proved to be unfeasible (at least for the immediate future, the first successful evaporation saltworks would not appear in New England until 1777), there still was a high demand for craftsmen skilled in the use of salt for packaging and shipping. Thus there existed an incredible opportunity for the first year-round salters to establish a trade in New England now that a permanent settlement had been established in the region.[81]

It is possible that Roger Conant met Thomas Weston during his time in London. Weston was, after all, scouring the city in search of potential settlers who had the appropriate skilled trades to make the Plymouth Colony profitable, and he certainly would have turned to the Salters Company in order to find a salter willing to emigrate. While it is impossible to say with any certainty what familiarity Roger Conant had with Thomas Weston, there does seem to be quite a bit of circumstantial evidence that they were colleagues of some sort. Roger Conant's son Johnathan would go on to marry Thomas Weston's daughter Elizabeth in Marblehead, Massachusetts, years after both men had passed. Both Roger Conant and Thomas Weston were in London during the same time, and while there is a record showing that Christopher Conant immigrated with his family to the Plymouth Colony aboard the *Anne*, arriving in June 1623,[82] there is no shipping manifest of Roger or Sarah Conant aboard any vessel. Yet around the time of Thomas Weston's arrival in Plymouth following the Wessagusett debacle, William Bradford began complaining about a nameless man

they sent to make salt…an ignorant, foolish, self-willed fellow. He bore them in hand, he could do great matters in making salt works, so he was sent to seek out fit ground for his purpose; and after some search he told the Governor that he had found a sufficient place, with a good bottom to hold water, and otherwise very convenient, which he doubted not but in a short time to bring to good perfection, and to yield them a great profit; but he must have eight or ten men to be constantly employed. He wished to be sure that the ground was good, and other things answerable, and that he could bring it to perfection; otherwise he would bring upon them a great charge by employing himself and so many men. But he was after some trial so confident as he caused them to send carpenters to rear a grate frame for a large house to receive the salt, and such other uses. But in the end all proved in vain, then he laid fault on the ground in which he was deceived; but if he might have the lighter to carry clay, he was sure he could do it.

Now the Governor and some other foresaw that this would come to little, yet they had so many malignant spirits among them, that would have laid it upon them in their letters of complaint to the Adventurers, as to their fault that would not suffer to go on, to bring his work to perfection. For as he by his bold confidence and large promises deceived them in England that sent him, so he had wound himself into these men's high esteem here, so as they were fain to let him go on till all men saw his vanity. For he could not do anything but boil salt in pans, and yet would make them that were joined with him believe there was so great a mystery in it as was not easy to be attained, and made them do many unnecessary things to blind their eyes till they discovered his subtlety. The next year he was sent to Cape Ann, and the pans were set up where the fishing was; but before the summer was out he burnt the house and the fire was so vehement as it spoiled the pans, at least some of them, and this was the end of that chargeable business.[83]

This "ignorant, foolish, self-willed" salter who "the next year was sent to Cape Ann" could be none other than Roger Conant. Indeed, by making "them that were joined with him believe there was so great a mystery in it as was not easy to be attained" this nameless salter was merely upholding the oath he swore to the Salters Company "to preserve the secrets of the Fellowship." It also seems from this passage that Roger Conant did attempt to make salt through evaporation before giving up and resorting to simply boiling seawater. Yet this raises a question: Why such animosity? William Bradford was quite meticulous in his record keeping, and it is curious that he would not even record Roger Conant's name in his history of the colony no matter how much he may have personally disliked the man. Bradford is blatantly dismissive of Conant's contributions in not only this passage but also throughout the rest of his writings on the colony. It is as if he was intentionally trying to write the man out of history. If Roger Conant and his family had arrived in Plymouth with Thomas Weston, spending a season first with the fishermen at Damariscove, Maine, and arrived shortly after the full scope of the Wessagusett tragedy came to a head, then this would explain not only the lack of any shipping manifest featuring Roger, Sarah and young Caleb Conant but also the instant animosity of William Bradford. Of course, this is simply speculation, but it is at least a rational assumption and the timing does align well with the events that were about to unfold.

5

PILGRIMS VERSUS STRANGERS

Conflict Within and Exodus from the Plymouth Colony

T he Conant brothers and their families weren't the only new arrivals at the Plymouth Colony in the spring of 1624. By the end of the year, the struggling colony would be the home of 180 residents.[84] Many, if not most, of these new arrivals were not the separatist "Saints" of the remaining Leyden Congregation in Holland like the rest of those Pilgrims who ruled the colony. Increasingly, these new arrivals were of the sort of people the Pilgrims referred to as "Strangers"—that is, somewhat less religiously inclined, members of the Church of England and generally either skilled tradesmen or servants in some form or another. Among these new Strangers were two men who would infuriate the Pilgrim Plymouth authorities to the point of causing the greatest rift yet between Saints and Strangers in the young settlement and who both would later prove to have close associations with Roger Conant: the Anglican Reverend John Lyford and John Oldham. Although Roger Conant is never mentioned in the controversy surrounding Lyford and Oldham, he did later move to Nantasket with them when they were banished by the Plymouth Colony toward the end of the summer of 1624, and Lyford would later go on to join Roger Conant at Cape Ann. Most of what is known about the Lyford-Oldham controversy comes, like much of the rest of the early history of the Plymouth and Massachusetts Colonies, from the writings of William Bradford, William Hubbard and Thomas Morton. Of these men, only Bradford and Morton write about the event in much detail, and only Bradford was actually present to both witness and play a leading

John Oldham. *Courtesy of the New York Public Library.*

a role in the events that followed. As such, William Bradford (who had assumed the role of governor upon the death of John Carver in 1620) remains the best source for the events that transpired that summer, so long as the reader remains critical of his blatant conflict of interest.

Until the arrival of the Reverend John Lyford, there had been no minister for the congregation at the Plymouth Colony. The Leyden Congregation's minister, John Robinson, had remained behind in Holland when the *Mayflower* sailed for the New World, and he had been unable to make passage since. The duties of a minister for the colony were taken up by the Elder William Brewster. According to William Bradford, Brewster had performed those duties quite well and much to the satisfaction of the Pilgrims. As a religious faith that emphasized a personal relationship with God, having an official minister was never seen as truly essential to maintaining a strong and faithful community, and indeed, nearly any member of the congregation could assist in serving in that role in some capacity. Brewster was an educated man and knowledgeable about matters of faith, which is why he had assumed the ministerial role in the community. While under the reign of King James I there was a great deal of wiggle room for Protestant teachings within the Church of England, it still remained the case that all citizens had to be members of the Church of England in a congregation that was under the teachings of a minister of the Church of England. The Plymouth Colony had no such minister, and the leader of the sect in Holland, the Reverend John Robinson, had been expelled by the Church of England. It is unclear whether or not John Lyford came to the Plymouth Colony in the "official" capacity as a minister of the Church of England, but he soon began to take on that role.

William Bradford writes extensively on how welcoming the colony was at first to the new Reverend Lyford, "but this lasted not long, for both Oldham and he grew very perverse, and showed signs of a great malignancy, drawing as many to faction as they could. Were they never so vile or profane, they did nourish and back them in all their doings, so they would cleave to them and speak ill of the church here."[85]

When a ship, the *Charity*, was readying for departure to England, Lyford was observed writing several letters to friends and associates back home. This raised a great deal of concern among the Pilgrims; after the ship departed, William Bradford and a few others set out in a shallop to intercept the ship, seize the letters and make copies of them to send back to England along with rebuttals to the charges leveled against the ruling Plymouth Colony authorities and church. The captain, William Pierce, cooperated with Bradford. This expedition was undertaken out of sight of the colony and was passed off as a fishing expedition to excuse the company's absence from the colony. Neither Lyford nor Oldham were confronted immediately about these letters. Instead, Bradford chose to wait "that they might better discover their intents and see who were their adherents."[86]

In these letters, it was revealed that John Lyford planned a reformation among the church in the colony and he was planning to take the sacraments with his followers. In addition to this papist and heathen ritual (at least to the Pilgrim mind, no matter that it was part of the doctrine of the more Protestant-leaning Church of England), Lyford accused the Pilgrim Plymouth Colony of a wide array of abuses against those "Strangers" who had come to settle at Plymouth at the hands of the local political and religious authorities. Among these accusations was that the ruling Pilgrims actively engaged in ostracizing both socially and politically Strangers who had come to settle there, hampered their economic progress, excluded them from civil government and even went so far as to provide them with fewer food stores than that which was given to the Pilgrims. Lyford also counseled the Merchant Adventurers who were financing the colony that they should do everything in their power to prevent the minister in Leyden Holland, John Robinson, from immigrating to the colony; Lyford feared what the consequences might be for those Strangers if that should happen. He also counseled that a new military leader should be sent over to relieve Myles Standish. Letters written by John Oldham were also deemed incriminating, but Bradford neglected to record copies of those, because "he was so bad a scribe as his hand was scarce legible, yet he was as deep in this mischief as the other."[87]

Tensions between the Lyford-Oldham faction and the Pilgrims quickly escalated. Though it remains unclear how much support Lyford had among the Strangers of the colony, it was at least enough to cause major concern for the Pilgrims. John Oldham got into an argument with Myles Standish that, according to William Bradford, stemmed from Oldham's refusal to stand watch and resulted in the newcomer pulling a knife on Standish. Bradford came in to restrain Oldham while he "ramped more like a furious beast than a man, and called them traitors and rebels and other such foul language as I am ashamed to remember." Shortly thereafter, Lyford began to withdraw his followers from the church on Sundays and hold services in the Anglican manner, with the sacraments, outdoors in full view of the Pilgrims. This was too much for Bradford, so he had Lyford and Oldham both arrested and charged with "disturbing their peace, both in respect of their civil and church state."[88]

At first, both John Lyford and John Oldham vehemently denied all of the charges leveled against them, and it was not until after hearing their denial that William Bradford produced the intercepted letters. John Oldham raged against his private correspondence being intercepted and read, and he shouted to those assembled, "Now show your courage! You have oft complained to me so and so. Now is the time, if you will do anything, I will stand by you!"[89] No one stepped forward to stand by Oldham, and Bradford turned his attention to John Lyford. After a reading of the letters, Lyford burst into tears and threw himself on the mercy of the Pilgrim "court," damning himself for his own pride and called himself a reprobate and unworthy of God's mercy. This was likely an act on Lyford's part, as he knew full well the value the Pilgrims, and the Puritans for that matter, placed on a public and "voluntary" confession of one's sins. Nearly every trial in seventeenth-century New England culminated in such a display. Gradually, more and more pressure would be brought to bear on the accused until it became obvious that a conviction was a foregone conclusion, at which point the accused was expected to confess all and throw themselves on the mercy of the assembled court. During the colony's early years, this court was really a public assembly of the congregation headed by an elder or the governor (in this case William Bradford) acting as both judge and prosecutor. How voluntary these confessions really were is quite obviously rather suspect. During the Salem Witch Trials in 1692, one accused witch, Giles Corey, refused to confess to witchcraft and so was pressed to death over the course of three days. Corey never confessed, but his death and others served as a warning to the rest of the community. Before long, John Oldham would learn that same lesson.

Both Oldham and Lyford were expelled from the colony. However, Oldham's wife and children were allowed to remain until he was able to arrange for suitable lodgings, and Lyford was allowed to remain for a maximum of six months. John Oldham, Roger Conant and a few others moved to Nantasket, where a small trading post had been established a year earlier to facilitate trade with the neighboring Massachusett. John Lyford, however, remained behind in Plymouth for the time being.

Sometime in the spring of 1624 (which William Bradford records as 1625 because the practice at that time was that years began and end in the springtime, hence 1625 began in April 1624), Oldham returned to visit the Plymouth Colony. It is not clear how long this was after his expulsion or what the purpose of his visit may have been. It is quite possible he was doing nothing more than paying a visit to his wife and children. At any rate, John Oldham was not given the chance to even state the purpose for his being there. Upon Oldham's approach, he was seized by William Pierce and Edward Winslow. Myles Standish then called out the guard to form two lines, each facing one another, with muskets and clubs in hand. Oldham was to be made to run the gauntlet. This was a brutal punishment. One man would lead Oldham through the gauntlet at sword point, standing in front of him with the sword pointed at his neck in order to prevent him from running through it so that the ordeal would proceed at a slow, deliberate pace. As Oldham passed each man in the gauntlet, he would have been clubbed or whipped. Anyone who shied away or delivered too light a blow would likewise be beaten. Yet those assembled there that day to beat Oldham probably didn't need much urging, for when they were done, they called out that Lyford should be next.[90]

But forcing a minister of the Church of England, even one who encouraged his followers to partake in the "papist" sacraments, to run the gauntlet was a bit extreme even for the Pilgrims, so a new trial for Lyford was held. Bradford opened the trial by quoting Psalms 7:15, "He hath made a pit and digged it, and is fallen into the pit he has made."[91] During this trial, John Lyford's wife was brought forth to testify against her husband. She accused him of having a bastard child back in England with another woman prior to their marriage that she was only made aware of after the wedding. She also testified that he had slept with her maids, and "some time she had taken him that manner, as they [the maids] lay at their bed's feet, with such other circumstances as I am ashamed to relate."[92] William Pierce and Edward Winslow both testified against Lyford that they had heard from some acquaintances back in England (how and from whom is not entirely clear) that controversy accompanied Lyford wherever he went. According to them, Lyford previously served as a priest in Ireland and had been forced to leave after raping a woman who was engaged, "though he satisfied his lust on her, yet he endeavored to hinder conception." This time, Lyford did have some defenders during the trial who cried out that witnesses to these events must be made present. (William Bradford doesn't bother to record who these defenders were.) More members of the congregation were brought in to testify, and Lyford was summarily expelled from the colony. Lyford joined Oldham, Conant and those other disgruntled Strangers at Nantasket.

While it is plausible that the Reverend John Lyford was a rapist, it's obvious that even by the rather low standards of seventeenth-century English legal proceedings, he did not receive a fair and impartial trial. Regardless of the accuracy of the claims leveled against him, clearly, John Lyford was perceived as serious threat to the control the Pilgrims wielded over the nascent Plymouth Colony. Why the Pilgrims were so intimidated by Oldham is never quite made clear—other than his association with Lyford, of course—but the threat that the Anglican reverend posed is glaringly obvious. Unlike any of the Pilgrims, Lyford was an ordained priest of the Church of England. Lyford preached and adhered to a faith that was not only the official faith of the Crown but also one that was rather popular among the somewhat more secular and tradition-loving Strangers. The Church of England tolerated the popular feast days and maypole dances and, despite all of its pomp and ceremony, was infinitely more liberal and tolerant of people's personal lives than the dour Pilgrims, who seemed to see sin in everything. The Pilgrims were in quite the bind. They were, after all, obligated to turn a profit for their investors, yet none of them had the requisite skills to do that in the New World. They were an urban people who had spent the decade leading up to their immigration mostly working in the mills of Holland's early textile industry. While their self-righteous determination was crucial to holding the colony together during those first years of famine and starvation, it has to be noted that as a congregation they simply lacked the skill set for those trades that would be most profitable for the new colony. They needed people skilled as carpenters, sailors, fishermen, salters, shipbuilders and farmers— trades that took years to master and were frankly sorely lacking among the Pilgrims. Those who did possess these requisite skills had to be recruited from elsewhere, mostly the West Country of England. Thus, many of these Strangers held a different, more traditional set of beliefs than the Pilgrims. Lyford's very presence upset that control that William Bradford and his Pilgrim contemporaries wielded over the young colony, and it should come as no surprise that he would be so targeted.

The most damning evidence against William Bradford for his prosecution of Lyford and Oldham comes from his own hand. Bradford almost gleefully writes of the actions he took to not only maintain Pilgrim control over the colony but also shape the perception of the colony by those back in

England and future generations. He was keenly conscious of the importance of perception to the success of their religious enterprise and took great strides to censor everything that could possibly be construed as critical of the Pilgrim authorities. Beyond intercepting private letters bound for England, Bradford made a conscious decision to preserve only those that he felt placed his opponents in the most negative light or placed him or his contemporaries in a positive light. Bradford meticulously preserved much of the correspondence from this period, yet his works are filled with references to other letters that, like Oldham's correspondence, he dismisses as tedious or irrelevant. These actions do provide some insight into his complete omission of Roger Conant, save of course for the dismissive description of a nameless salter. One would think that the man who would go on to become the first governor of the second successful colony of New England would merit *some* passing reference at least, but such is not the case in Bradford's history. In writing his history, he even goes so far as to refer to himself in the third person by his title, relating on and on about the difficult decisions the governor had to make or the brave actions the governor had to take to ensure peace, prosperity and tranquility. William Bradford *was* the governor, but he writes as though he was the governor's cheerleader rather than the governor himself.

Perhaps the most bizarre part of William Bradford's narrative comes from the alleged confession of John Oldham. Bradford relates a story that sometime after this incident, John Oldham took passage on a ship bound for Virginia and got caught in a storm off Cape Cod:

> But it so pleased God that the bark that carried him and many other passengers was in that danger that they despaired of life; so as many of them, as they fell to prayer, so also did they begin to examine their consciences and confess such sins as did most burden them. And Mr. Oldham did make a free and large confession of the wrongs he had done to the people and church here, in many particulars, that as he had sought their ruin, so God had now met with him and might destroy him; yea, he feared they all fared the worse for his sake. He prayed God to forgive him and made vows that if the Lord spared his life he would become otherwise, and the like. This I had from some of good credit.[93]

That confession that Bradford so wanted from Oldham finally came—some unknown time later, during some unknown storm, on an unknown ship, but we can rest assured that it was a factual and true confession. After all, it was related to Bradford by some unknown source whom he assures us is of "good credit." Yet exactly what Oldham confessed or what his crimes against the Pilgrims were remains a mystery. Whatever he wrote back to England has been lost, and Bradford only managed to recall that one incident where Oldham got into a confrontation with Myles Standish, allegedly over Oldham's refusal to stand watch. Whatever else Oldham needed to confess in the eyes of William Bradford has been lost to history. It seems as though that in his zeal to press forward with the prosecution, Bradford neglected to mention the crime. Perhaps that fact tells us all we need to know about the reasons Roger Conant and other Strangers like him had for leaving the Plymouth Colony to make a new home in this New World.

6

A NEW COLONY ESTABLISHED AND
A CIVIL WAR AVERTED

The Settlement of Cape Ann and the Invasion of
the Cape Ann Colony by the Plymouth Colony

I t is likely no small coincidence that William Bradford and the Pilgrims'
nearly fanatical obsession with controlling the flow of information back
to England coincided with a renewed push to expand their influence over
a wider swath of what would become Massachusetts. In 1623, the Plymouth
Colony obtained a patent from Lord Sheffield to erect a fishing station at
Cape Ann. That Lord Sheffield had at this time also issued a patent to the
Dorchester Company for the same enterprise at the same location seems to
have mattered little to him. As the Plymouth Colony was already operating in
North America, they were the first to be able to establish a presence on Cape
Ann and rushed to make improvements on the property there in order to lay
a more permanent claim to it. In March 1623, Edward Winslow took a few
Plymouth settlers and supplies aboard the ship *Charity* to begin establishing a
satellite colony for Plymouth at Cape Ann. It was during this expedition that
the fishing stage that would later be a source of such contention between
the Dorchester Company and the Plymouth Colony was constructed, along
with a saltworks and "a great frame house."[94]

Unfortunately for the Plymouth Colony, the attempt at setting up a fishery
at Cape Ann met with complete disaster. A fire destroyed the saltworks and
damaged the great house, the soil quality at the cape proved to be far too
sandy for planting any crops that might sustain the colony and the one
fishing vessel employed in the area by the Plymouth Colony failed to make
any real profitable voyage. In 1624, the Crown appointed a man named
Christopher Levett admiral over the coasts of New England. Levett was

Historical marker for the Cape Ann Colony at Stage Fort Park, Gloucester, Massachusetts. *Photo by author.*

charged with regulating fishing and trade and enforcing the Crown's policies on the water in this new territory. Ultimately, this proved to be a fool's errand, as the Crown had neither the capability nor the interest to invest the huge amount of naval power that would be required to undertake such an endeavor. Thus, Christopher Levett's time as admiral of New England was short-lived. However, he did make an observation of Cape Ann at this time that was rather poignant. In a report back to England, Levett wrote,

> *But it seems they have no fish to make benefit of, for this year they had one ship fish in Pemoquid, and another at Cape Ann, where they have begun a new Plantation, but how long it will continue I know not. I fear there hath been too fair a gloss set on Cape Ann. I am told there is a good harbor which makes a fair invitation, but when they are in, their entertainment is not answerable, for there is little good ground, and the ships which fished there this year, their boats went twenty miles to take their fish, and yet they were in great fear of not making their voyages, as one of the masters confessed unto me who was at my house.[95]*

The Charter for the North Shore of Massachusetts Bay

Known as the Sheffild Patent

THIS INDENTURE made the first day of January Anno Dni 1623, And in the Yeares of the Raigne of o' Soveraigne Lord James by the grace of God King of England ffrance and Ireland Defender of the ffaith &c the One and Twentyth And of Scotland the Seaven and ffyftyth BETWEENE the right honorable Edmond Lord Sheffeild Knight of the most noble Order of the Garter on thone parte and Robert Cushman and Edward Winslowe for themselves, and theire Associats and Planters at Plymouth in New England in America on thother part. WYTNESSETH that the said Lord Sheffeild (As well in consideracon that the said Robert and Edward and divers of theire Associats haue already adventured themselves in person, and haue likewise at theire owne proper Costs and Charges transported dyvers persons into New England aforesaid And for that the said Robert and Edward and their Associats also intend as well to transport more persons as also further to plant at Plymouth aforesaid, and in other places in New England aforesaid As for the better Advancement and furtherance of the said Planters, and encouragement of the said Vnderlakers) Hath Gyven, granted, assigned, allotted, and appointed And by these pnts doth Gyve, graunt, assigne, allott, and appoint vnto and for the said Robert and Edward and their Associats As well a certaine Tract of Ground in New England aforesaid lying in fortythree Degrees or thereabout of Northerly latitude and in a knowne place there comonly called Cape Anne, Together with the free vse and benefit as well of the Bay comonly called the Bay of Cape Anne, as also of the Islands within the said Bay And free liberty, to ffish, fowle, hawke, and hunt, truck, and trade in the Lands thereabout, and in all other places in New England aforesaid; whereof the said Lord Sheffeild is, or hath byn possessed, or which haue byn allotted to him the said Lord Sheffeild, or within his Jurisdiccon (not nowe being inhabited, or hereafter to be inhabited by any English) Together also with ffyve hundred Acres of free Land adioyning to the said Bay to be ymployed for publiq vses, as for the building of a Towne, Scholes, Churches, Hospitalls, and for the mayntenance of such Ministers, Officers, and Magistrats, as by the said vndertakers, are there already appointed, or which hereafter shall (with theire good liking, reside, and inhabitt there And also Thirty Acres of Land, over and beside the ffyve hundred Acres of Land, before mencoved To be allotted, and appointed for every perticuler person, Young, or old (being the Associats, or servants of the said vndertakers or their successo" that shall come, and dwell at the aforesaid Cape Anne within Seaven yeares next after the Date hereof, which Thirty

Acres of Lande soe appointed to every person as aforesaid, shall be taken as the same doth lye together vpon the said Bay in one entire place, and not stragling in dyvers, or remote parcells not exceeding an English Mile, and a halfe in length on the Waters side of the said Bay YELDING AND PAYING for ever yearely vnto the said Lord Sheffeild, his heires, successo", Rent gatherer, or assignes for every Thirty Acres soe to be obteyned, and possessed by the said Robert & Edward theire heires, successo", or Associats Twelve Pence of lawfull English money At the ffeast of St. Michaell Tharchangell only (if it be lawfully demaunded) The first payment thereof To begynne ymediately from and aiter thend and expiracon of the first Seaven yeares next after the date hereof AND THE SAID Lord Sheffeild for himself his heires, successo", and assignes doth Covenant, promise, and graunt to and with the said Robert Cushman, and Edward Winslow their heires associats, and assignes That they the said Robert, and Edward, and such other persons as shall plant, and contract with them, shall freely and quyetly, haue, hold, possesse, and enioy All such profitts, rights, previlidges, benefits, Comodities, advantages, and prehemineces, as shall hereafter by the labo", search, and diligence of the said Vndertakers their heires, associats, servants, or Assignes be obteyned, found out, or made within the said Tract of Ground soe graunted vnto them as aforesaid; Reserving vnto the said Lord Sheffeild his heires, successors, and assignes The one Moyety of all such Mynes as shall be discovered, or found out at any tyme by the said Vndertakers, or any their heires, successo", or assignes vpon the Grounds aforesaid AND further That it shall and may be lawfull to and for the said Robert Cushman, and Edward Winslowe their heires, associats, and assignes from tyme to tyme, and at all tymes hereafter soe soone or they or their Assignes haue taken possession, or entred into any of the said Lands To forbyd, repell, repulse and resist by force of Armes All and every such persons as shall build, plant, or inhabitt, or which shall offer, or make shew to build, plant, or inhabitt within the Lands soe as aforesaid graunted, without the leave, and consent of the said Robert, and Edward or theire assignes AND THE SAID Lord Sheffeild doth further Covenant, and graunt That vpon a lawfull survey hadd, and taken of the aforesaid Lands, and good informacon gyven to the said Lord Sheffeild his heires, or assignes, of the Meats, Bounds, and quantity of Lands which the said Robert, and Edward their heires, associates, or assignes shall take in and be by them their Associats, Servants, or Assigns inhabited as aforesaid; the said Lord Sheffeild his heires, or assigns, at and vpon

the reasonable request of the said Vndertakers, or theire Associats, shall and will by good and sufficient Assurance in the Lawe Graunt, enfeoffe, confirm and allott vnto the said Robert Cushman and Edward Winslowe theire Associats, and Assigns All and every the said Lands soe to be taken in within the space of Seaven yeares next after the Date hereof in as larg, ample, and beneficiall manner, as the said Lord Sheffeild his heires, or assignes nowe haue, or hereafter shall have the same Lands, or any of them graunted unto him, or them; for such rent, and vnder such Covenants, and Provisoes as herein are conteyned (mutatis mutandis) AND shall and will also at all tymes hereafter vpon reasonable request made to him the said Lord Sheffeild his heires, or assignes by the said Edward and Robert their heires, associats, or assignes, or any of them, graunt, procure, and make good, lawfull, and sufficient Letters, or other Graunts of Incorporacon whereby the said Vndertakers, and their Associats shall haue liberty and lawfull authority from tyme to tyme to make and establish Lawes, Ordynnces, and Constitucons for the ruling, ordering, and governing of such persons as now are resident, or which hereafter shalbe planted, and inhabitt there And in the meane tyme vntill such Graunt be made It shalbe lawfull for the said Robert, and Edward their heires, associats and Assignes by consent of the greater part of them to Establish such Lawes, Provisions and Ordynnces as are or shalbe by them thought most fitt, and convenient for the governement of the said plantacon which shall be from tyme to tyme executed, and administred by such Officer, or Officers, as the said Vndertakers, or their Associats or the most part of them shall elect, and make choice of PROVYDED allwaies That the said Lawes, Provisions, and Ordynnces which are, or shall be agreed on, be not repugnant to the Lawes of England, or to the Orders, and Constitucons of the President and Councell of New England PROVYDED further That the said Vndertakers theire heires, and successo" shall fore" acknowledg the said Lord Sheffeild his heires and successo", to be theire Chiefe Lord, and to answeare and doe service vnto his Lo^p or his Successo", at his, or theire Court when vpon his, or theire owne Plantacon The same shalbe established, and kept IN WYTNES whereof the said parties to these present Indentures Interchaungeably have putt their Hands and Seals The day and yeares first abone written.

SHEFFEYLD.

Seal pendent.

Sheffield Patent. *Courtesy of the Library of Congress.*

By the close of 1624, the Plymouth Colony had abandoned the effort at Cape Ann. Whether or not the colonists intended to return and try for another attempt later is pure speculation. However, they definitely felt that despite abandoning the property, they still retained a claim over it. The Plymouth Colony interpreted its patent from Lord Sheffield to mean that any people peacefully employed at Cape Ann tacitly acknowledged Plymouth's claim to the region by virtue of the fact that Plymouth would only admit those who did to settle there or use the facilities. It is a quite bizarre line of legal logic: because *they* wouldn't accept anyone who didn't agree to *their* ownership of the property, anyone using the property therefore must accept that *they* own it. The Pilgrims took this view from that part of their patent for the region that authorized anyone who was either a planter (meaning settler) or anyone who was the *associate* of a planter to take up residence on the site. Plymouth therefore just took the position that anyone who later arrived at the site who wasn't one of their own planters must automatically therefore be agreeing to be an associate of a planter. These associates were thus more akin to guests or servants than they settlers of a location with an actual valid and legal claim to the property.[96] Plymouth just took this position as a fact rather than a speculation, and in a place where borders were questionable and courts nonexistent, for all intents and purposes it was. After all, the Plymouth Colony was settled somewhat illegally, as it had obtained a patent that only authorized settlement much farther south of where it ended up, yet the settlers managed to still retain ownership of the settlement by simply surviving. This was the New World, and as such, there were new ways of doing things.

Regardless of whatever designs the Plymouth Colony had for Cape Ann, the Dorchester Company began construction of its colony at Cape Ann in earnest in the autumn of 1624. The company may have even begun construction of its own fishing stages and buildings while some of the Plymouth colonists were still present at the site. In the mid-1620s, James I began to grow ill, and the ascension of the more Catholic-leaning—and therefore even more thoroughly anti-Puritan—Charles I to the throne became apparent. Against this backdrop, several prominent Puritans began to take a new look at New England, with the idea of setting up a permanent settlement as a potential refuge for Puritans that could be financially supported by fishing. With this in mind, two prominent Puritans within the Church of England—Arthur Lake, the Bishop of Bath, and the Reverend John White of Dorchester—began to approach various West Country merchants around Dorchester, England. The idea seemed a profitable one, and soon the merchants and reverends had organized themselves into a joint stock company, the Dorchester Company, with assets of more than £3,000, to establish a new colony at Cape Ann. Lord Sheffield, who always seemed agreeable to issuing patents to anyone who either had the funds or would be willing to make binding promises to pay in the future, promptly issued the new Dorchester Company a patent to settle in the region. The Dorchester Company appointed Thomas Gardner to oversee the construction of the new plantation and John Tylly to manage the fisheries and dispatched them to Cape Ann along with a few other settlers.[97]

The winter of 1624–25 found Roger, Sarah and Caleb Conant welcoming a new baby boy named Lot into their family at Nantasket. In January, Roger Conant received a letter from Reverend White that offered him the position of governor over the Cape Ann Colony on behalf of the Dorchester Company, which would "commit unto him the charge of all their affairs, as well as fishing and planting."[98] Reverend Lyford was likewise offered the position of minister over the nascent colony, and John Oldham was offered the opportunity to manage the colony's trade with the Natives in the region. Both Lyford and Conant immediately accepted the offer and made arrangements to move their families to Cape Ann, while Oldham decided to try his luck with fur trading on his own, at least for a while. Thus, Roger Conant became the first governor of Massachusetts—at least in a sense. Massachusetts as a geopolitical body did not quite exist at this time and would not exist for another four years, when John Endicott, the first official governor of Massachusetts, arrived in Salem in 1629. It also should be noted that while the title of governor does indeed sound like a political office to modern ears, it would be more accurate to describe Roger Conant's position as more of a manager or an overseer. After all, he had received his position from a private company rather than from the Crown or any political entity, and he was charged with overseeing and managing the affairs of that colony on behalf of that private company rather than the British Crown. Yet on the far side of the world thousands of miles beyond the reach of any real governmental authority, he defiantly served in the capacity of a governor in the very real and modern sense of the word. For Cape Ann at least, Roger Conant was pretty much the only readily accessible authority around. It also must be said that other than a commission and a title, the Dorchester Company gave Conant nothing with which to enforce his authority. No soldiers would be present to enforce the will of the governor on any who might disagree—just a motley collection of fishermen, planters and a rather dubious priest who were simply expected to accept the rule of Conant on behalf of the company.

Exactly why Reverend White chose Roger Conant for the position of governor remains a little unclear. It is possible that the two men knew each other in England. Dorchester is not all that far from East Budleigh in Devon, where Roger Conant grew up, but that is simply pure speculation. It is also possible that they knew of each other through the Salters Company. In any case, the financers of the Dorchester Company appear to have been well satisfied with Conant's qualifications, experience and capabilities. Given the Plymouth Colony governor's penchant for seizing and censoring correspondence between New England and England, there must have been some other method of communication across the Atlantic. It is likely that correspondence was carried by the many fishermen who regularly made such voyages and whose expeditions were also often underwritten by some of the same West Country merchants who were shareholders in the Dorchester Company. Exactly what their take on the recent events in the Plymouth Colony regarding Lyford and Oldham was is a mystery, but given that they offered Lyford, Oldham and that nameless salter Conant positions of authority in their new £3,000 endeavor indicates that they had a significantly different interpretation of those events than William Bradford relates.

By the spring of 1625, Roger Conant had moved to Cape Ann and taken over coordination of the operation there. Much of the needed infrastructure, such as the fishing stage, some saltworks and at least one large clapboard house, had already been constructed in previous years, and while several of these works had been damaged in a fire, it wouldn't have taken all that much work to get them repaired and useable again. Fishermen had also already begun visiting and using the site on their own rather frequently. Yet while the fishing station was definitely beginning to show signs of improvement, it was almost immediately apparent to Roger Conant that the site was completely unsuitable for a colony. The problem lay with the soil, which remains to this day extremely poor, sandy, rocky and strewn with boulders. Hardly any portion of it was suitable for growing the crops that would be needed for the survival of the colonists. Thus Conant began almost immediately to search for a site that would be more suitable.

Just a few miles west of Cape Ann lay a site where two large rivers forked before entering into a wide bay surrounded by numerous sheltered harbors. While like Cape Ann the landscape was quite rocky, the silt deposits from the rivers had left wide expanses of fertile soil, which the Massachusett had previously cleared for small-scale horticulture. In addition to this shore, fish were so abundant in the area that the Massachusett had named it Naumkeag, which is Algonquin for "good fishing place." This was the same place where less than a decade earlier John Smith had reported seeing thousands of Natives trading with French traders while he was exploring the coast. Yet only a few dozen Massachusett remained there now, and they were holed up in just a few small fortified villages scattered about the area—the last survivors of the catastrophic diseases and Tarrantine raids that had periodically swept the region in recent years.

Naumkeag appeared to Conant to be the perfect location for a new colony, and indeed it soon would become the first successful colony in Massachusetts (the Plymouth Colony being under an independent patent and therefore would not become part of Massachusetts until its charter was revoked in 1692) and is known today as Salem Sound. However, the founding of Salem would have to wait. Reverend White wrote to Conant that he "grieved in his spirit that so good a work should be suffered to fall to the ground."[99] The Dorchester Company insisted to Roger Conant that the Cape Ann site should not be so quickly abandoned after all the financial resources that had already been poured in to that colony's founding. Conant remained convinced that the Cape Ann Colony would have to be abandoned due to poor soil quality, but for the time being, he worked to accommodate the wishes of his employers.

Yet despite the poor soil, the harsh climate and all the other myriad threats that faced any attempt to establish a colony in New England at this time, the first serious threat that Roger Conant faced would come from other Englishmen. Choosing to take a literal view of that provision in their patent for Cape Ann that authorized them to "forbyd, repell, and repulse by force of arms"[100] any intrusion upon their possession, the Plymouth Colony decided to send an armed expedition under Myles Standish to evict the Dorchester Company's settlers from Cape Ann in June 1625. By this time, Governor William Bradford and the rest of the Plymouth Colony authorities had become quite adept at alternating between liberal and literal interpretations of their patent depending on which interpretation suited their needs at any given time. By taking the liberal and expansive interpretation of the provision that authorized only those who were either planters or associates of the Plymouth Colony to settle at the site and combining it with the provision to use force to repel any intruders, the Plymouth authorities felt that they had a legal justification to launch a military attack on another English colony in the region—or at least felt that they could make a compelling legal argument that they did.

As Myles Standish gathered his men for the expedition, the residents of the Cape Ann Colony were going about the business they had come to the region to perform. A West Country fisherman named Captain Hewes had recently arrived in Cape Ann with a ship full of freshly caught cod, and he and his men were busy on the fishing stage filleting and laying out the cod to dry in preparation for packing the dried cod into barrels of salt for shipment back to England. Another West Country fisherman, Captain Pierse, was still aboard his ship in the harbor making preparations to unload his cargo so that they too could begin the process of drying their cod on the fishing stages of Cape Ann. With such a small population and such an abundance of freshly caught cod, the unloading, filleting and drying of the cod would have been a community affair employing nearly everyone in the colony to make sure the work was done quickly before the fish spoiled. Men, along with some women and children, dressed in shabby work smocks and wide-brimmed hats to block out the sun, frantically cleaned the cod with sharp blades and tossed aside the offal before laying the fillets in neat rows on the wooden stage to dry in the sun and wind. It would have been smelly and tedious work, yet the arrival of new fishermen who, like the settlers, had for months not seen any new faces must have led to some banter as the two groups swapped stories and relayed what little news they had to one another. When they first saw a new sail on the horizon approaching from the south, they likely assumed it was simply some other fishermen coming to dry and salt their catch and likely felt a mixture of jubilation that their new colony was bringing in so much work and exhausted frustration at the thought of having to gut, fillet and dry yet another ship full of cod. When that new ship launched a boat full of armed men and made for the shore, the alarm went up.

Captain Hewes ordered his men to erect a barricade of barrels, crates and whatever else they could lay their hands on to protect his catch on the fishing stage. Those fish represented the culmination of months of hard work at sea and a great deal of financial investment. If he and his men lost the catch before it could be sold back in England, they, like any fishermen who returned from a voyage empty-handed, would all face certain financial ruin. Peering over their hastily erected fortification, the fishermen watched as about a dozen men armed with matchlock muskets began the climb from the beach up the slope to confront them. That those armed men were plainly Englishmen and had disembarked from an English ship was likely confusing to the fishermen, who made ready to defend their livelihoods, but they weren't going to take any chances. As the armed party grew closer, it is likely that some of the men began to recognize Myles Standish or perhaps some of the other men advancing toward them, but it is doubtful that recognition offered the fishermen assembled any assurances.

As the party under Myles Standish approached the stage, they demanded that the fishermen cease using those works, over which the Plymouth Colony claimed ownership. A heated exchange ensued between two armed parties, and it must have seemed that both sides would come to blows. In a letter to the Earl of Arundel written on July 1, 1625, David Thompson called for the removal of William Bradford as governor of the Plymouth Colony. Thompson also claimed to be present on Cape Ann that day:

> *This yeere there hardlie escaped great murder & bloodshed, at Cape Anne for stage roome. 16 or 17 muskateers came from Newplymth, bothe pties seemed not only resolute but desperat. By good fortune I was there accidently, and used many argumnt on bothe sydes to dissuade such ungodlie, violent & unanswerable prceedings. The daye & tyme, yea place, appointed to fight, on shoare. Barricades & Bulw'kes made. Shippes readie, not to faylle to*

playe their pts. These are the fruits of unrulie multitudes. The last yeere they scoft the gouvernor & his authoritie becaus he wanted power.[101]

While writing of the event years later, William Hubbard (who would years later immigrate to Ipswich, Massachusetts; became a friend of Roger Conant; and likely heard the story from him) attacked both Myles Standish's height and the Pilgrims' blatant and hypocritical lack of Christian virtue by resorting to the use of force:

> *Captain Standish had been bred a soldier in the Low Countries, and never entered the school of our Savior Christ, or of John the Baptist, his harbinger, or, if he was ever there, forgot his first lessons, to offer violence to no man, and to part with the cloak rather than needlessly contend for the coat, though taken away without order. A little chimney is soon fired; so was the Plymouth Captain, a man of very little stature, yet of a very hot and angry temper. The fire of his passion soon kindled and blown up into a flame by hot words, might easily have consumed all, had it not been seasonably quenched.*[102]

The person that "seasonably quenched" Myles Standish's "passion" was none other than Roger Conant, who, along with Captain Pierse, prevented the argument from escalating to violence. Exactly what words were exchanged or how long the negotiations lasted remain unclear. David Thompson may indeed have also played a role in negotiating the peace that day, but if he did, no one else seems to have taken any note of it. Regardless of the details of the negotiations, it seems apparent that Myles Standish saw his position as untenable given that he and his armed force were now facing a fortification manned by determined fishermen and that there were two vessels in the harbor that could oppose him and potentially cut off his retreat. Standish may even have been counting on Captain Pierse siding with him in this confrontation. This was, after all, the same Captain Pierse who had enjoyed a positive relationship with the Plymouth Colony in the past and even assisted in the apprehension of Reverend John Lyford and John Oldham by the Plymouth Colony authorities a year earlier. At any rate, for all the bravado and brandishing of arms, Myles Standish was finding himself in an increasingly difficult position.

The agreement Roger Conant mediated between the fishermen and the Plymouth force was rather anticlimactic in the end. Conant, the fishermen and the Cape Ann Colony agreed to construct a new fishing stage, exclusively for the use of the Plymouth Colony, if Myles Standish and his men would leave. This was quite obviously little more than an olive branch to allow Myles Standish to save face and thus "quench" his "passion." Yet as inconsequential as this compromise appeared to be, it did once and for all firmly establish the Dorchester Company's claim over Cape Ann in the face of the Plymouth Colony's recent aggression. The Plymouth Colony had, by not pressing the issue to a violent conclusion, tacitly conceded that the Dorchester Company's settlement on Cape Ann did indeed have a right to exist independently of the Pilgrim's authority.

It should come as no surprise that William Bradford's interpretation of the events in June 1625 was quite different than William Hubbard's version. In his history of the Plymouth Colony, William Bradford wrote,

> *But some of Lyford's and Oldham's friends and their adherents set out a ship on fishing on their own account, and getting the start of the ships that came to the plantation, they took away their stage and other necessary provisions that they had made for fishing at Cape Ann the year before, at their great charge, and would not restore the same, except they would fight for it. But the Governor sent some of the planters to help the fishermen build a new one, and so let them keep it.*[103]

Once again, the real culprits in Bradford's eyes were his old nemeses John Lyford and John Oldham, and he refuses to name Roger Conant, although he does at least acknowledge the role the "governor" played in deescalating the hostilities. It is also interesting to note that William Bradford makes no mention of Myles Standish or of the armed party of musketeers that could only have been dispatched to Cape Ann under his orders, as he was serving as governor of the Plymouth Colony at the time of this incident. Perhaps Bradford legitimately did not think this incident merited all that much attention in his history of the Plymouth Colony; indeed, he devotes only five pages to the entire year of 1625–26. It definitely appears as if he was trying carefully to paint the Plymouth Colony as anything but the aggressor and perhaps even as the recipient of foul treatment at the hands of the Dorchester Company settlers. The fact that he sent an armed party to forcibly evict the Dorchester Company settlers wouldn't exactly play well into that narrative, so he conveniently left that out of his history. It should also be noted that William Bradford wrote his history at a time when the fate of the Plymouth Colony as a colony independent of the rapidly growing and influential Massachusetts Bay Colony was in question (and indeed soon thereafter the Plymouth Colony would be absorbed into the Massachusetts Bay Colony), and he may have been overly sensitive of appearing aggressive toward the founders of Massachusetts during their early days of settlement.

Yet as inconsequential as the incident on Cape Ann might have appeared to be to William Bradford in his history of the colony, it was important enough at the time of the event to dispatch Myles Standish to England to press the Plymouth Colony's claim over the area. In a letter dated June 28, 1625, to the Council of New England, carried personally by Myles Standish across the Atlantic, William Bradford wrote,

> *They have not only cast us off, but entered into a particular course of trading, and have by violence and force, taken at their pleasure our possession at Cape Anne. Traducing us with unjust and dishonest clamors abroad, disturbing our peace at home, and some of them threatening, that if ever we know a good estate, they will then nip us in the head. Which discouragements do cause us to slack our diligence and care to build and plant, and cheerfully perform other employments, not knowing for whom we work, whether friends or enemies.*
>
> *Our humble suit therefore to your good lordships and honors is, that seeing they have so unjustly forsaken us, that you would vouchsafe to convene them before you, and take such order, as we may be free from them; and they come to a division with us, that we and ours may be delivered from their evil intents against us. So shall we comfortably go forward with the work we have in hand, as first to God's glory, and the honor of our king; so to the good satisfaction of your honors, and for our present, common, and after goof of our posterity. The prosecution of this, we have committed to our agent Captain Myles Standish, who attends your Honorable pleasures.*[104]

The Council of New England either never considered the Plymouth Colony's claim to Cape Ann, or simply rejected it outright. William Bradford blamed this on the plague that had swept London that year, "for there was no courts kept, nor scarce any commerce held, the city being is a sort of desolate, by the fervent pestilence, and the flight of so many."[105] There indeed was a great plague that swept London in 1625–26 (as periodically happened to the city in the seventeenth century) and Bradford may well have been correct in his assessment. The council may also simply have chosen not to receive Myles Standish, given that the same year, in March 1625, James I passed away. The less Protestant friendly Charles I sat on the throne of England. With the new political reality, it may have been considered unwise to favor an audience with a representative of a radical Protestant sect regarding a claim against markedly less religiously fanatic West Country fishermen. In addition to the uncertain political realities of the new king, prominent members of the Council of New England, such as the Earl of Arundel, had for some time been receiving alarming reports about the authorities of the Plymouth Colony from the likes of David Thompson (whose letter to the earl regarding the incident at Cape Ann would have likely arrived around the same time Myles Standish did), Admiral Christopher Levett and others. Either way, the Plymouth Colony's claim was not heard, and by default, the Dorchester Company retained its legal right to settle and operate a new colony at Cape Ann. Myles Standish returned to the Plymouth Colony in April 1626 bearing not only the disheartening news of the loss of their claim to Cape Ann, the death of King James I and the ascension of Charles I to the throne but also of the loss of John Robinson, the Leyden Congregation's minister in Holland, whom they had been expecting to immigrate to lead the congregation in the New World, and Robert Cushman, a member of the Leyden Congregation who had remained in London to press the colony's interests at home.[106]

7

FAILURE AND OPPORTUNITY

*The Abandonment of the Cape Ann Colony and the
Establishment of the Colony at Naumkeag*

W hile the threat that the Cape Ann Colony faced from the
Plymouth Colony may have subsided, the Cape Ann colonists
still faced several challenges. Despite a successful fishing season,
events in Europe would soon turn the efforts of the colonists and their
investors into a complete financial disaster. In 1625, England waded into the
brutal religious conflict that had been raging over the European continent
between Protestant and Catholic nations since 1618 known as the Thirty
Years' War. During this conflict, England lent considerable support to the
Protestant French rebels known as the Huguenots and would eventually lay
siege to the French port of La Rochelle. France and Spain responded to this
aggression by barring all imports of English goods, including salt cod, from
their mainland ports. For the colonists of Cape Ann, these political reverses
could not have come at a worse time. The Dorchester Company was already
running on a tight budget. In 1625, the company borrowed £1,000 to outfit
the most recent fishing expedition to New England. The 1625 expeditions
had gotten off to a late start in the season and subsequently returned to
Europe not only much later than the rest of the English fishing fleet but also
completely ignorant of the political developments on the mainland. Finding
their salt cod barred from sale in both France and Spain (two nations that
normally imported huge quantities of salt cod), the Dorchester Company's
men sailed for England to attempt to salvage what profit they could for the
year. The Dorchester Company fishermen returned home to find the cod

market completely glutted with an overabundance of salt cod, so much so that the company just barely broke even on the loan it had taken out to finance the expedition. While the company had originally anticipated a minimum gross revenue for the expedition of at least £2,000 based on the return from previous expeditions, in the end it netted only £1,100 in revenue from salt cod sales. In order to meet other financial obligations, the Dorchester Company was even compelled to sell off one of its vessels for a substantial loss. The ship, which had been originally purchased for £1,200, was sold that year for a paltry £480. At the same time, the operating costs of the settlement at Cape Ann for the past two years had cost the Dorchester Company £1,000 per year and had failed to return any considerable profit for the company. By 1626, the Dorchester Company had folded.[107]

Of course, given the incredible amount of time it took for news to travel across the North Atlantic, the Cape Ann Colony remained unaware of the financial problems that its parent company was facing for quite some time. For them, the order of the day was survival, fishing and salting fish—and survival was proving exceedingly difficult. As Roger Conant had predicted, the staple crops were not taking to the sandy soil of Cape Ann, and though it is not mentioned, it is likely that this problem was further compounded by the cattle that had been brought to the site in 1624. Livestock, especially cattle, consume enormous quantities of grass, and given that the soil quality of Cape Ann was poor to begin with, it is more than likely that by 1625 the cattle had stripped the grass from what little topsoil existed. This would have caused substantial erosion. Until the mid-twentieth century, sheep and cattle grazed freely over various parts of Cape Ann, and the environmental damage from this practice can still be seen all over the cape to this day. Beginning in the early eighteenth century, poor members of the communities of Gloucester and Rockport began to settle in the region known as Dogtown Common (which lies roughly halfway between the two towns) and desperately tried to hack a living out of poor rocky soil amid grazing sheep. While Dogtown Common was abandoned as a settlement by the 1820s, the damage caused by this over-farming and grazing can still be seen today. The forest that once covered the area has since started to grow back, but one can easily see exposed ancient roots and boulders that have been left polished and exposed from the loss of so much topsoil. Likewise, areas of Cape Ann described by Samuel de Champlain as sandy beaches (such as Whale Cove, where Champlain made his first landfall) are now nearly completely devoid of sand and little more than exposed rock and pebbles. Islands just offshore in Champlain's time that were tree-covered are today

Thatcher's Island at Sunset. The island off the coast of Cape Ann was clear-cut shortly after the arrival of Europeans. Four hundred years later, trees have still been unable to grow there. *Photo by author.*

nearly completely barren despite the fact that there hasn't been any logging in the area since the eighteenth century.[108] By comparison, Misery Island in nearby Salem Sound is today completely forested despite the fact that the forest there was nearly entirely destroyed by a massive fire as recently as the 1920s. The difference between the locations is both the quality of soil and the exposure to the harsh weather of the North Atlantic. Misery Island lies in Salem Sound, a sheltered bay that is fed by numerous rivers and creeks and is protected from the harsh North Atlantic winds, whereas Cape Ann and its surrounding islands are completely exposed to some of the worst weather that the North Atlantic has to offer. Clearly, Roger Conant and those early settlers at Cape Ann faced some serious difficulties when trying to get staple European crops to take to the poor souls of Cape Ann.

Incredibly, despite the difficulty in planting crops and the harsh New England winter, there is no record of any loss of life on the Cape Ann Colony during the winter of 1625–26. Both of the Conant children (the only children we have a record of being present at the colony that year), Caleb (age three) and Lot (not even a year old), survived that winter, and if any other Cape Ann colonists passed away that season no record was ever made of it. This is in stark contrast to the experiences of the Plymouth colonists (who lost nearly half their number during their first winter in the New World) and the Wessagusset colonists (who didn't even survive one winter), and this alone is an incredible accomplishment and a testament to Roger Conant's leadership of the nascent colony. Meanwhile, back in England some of the members of the Dorchester Company laid the blame for the colony's failure to turn a profit squarely on the shoulders of Roger Conant. The Reverend John White, who had solicited Conant for the position of governor and who had up until now been one of Roger Conant's solid backers back in England, wrote in the "Planter's Plea":

> *Unto these losses by fishing were added two other no small disadvantages: the one in the country by our landsmen, who being ill chosen and commanded, fell into many disorders and did the company little service; the other by the fall of the price of shipping.*

Despite the disparaging comments on Roger Conant's leadership and conduct to peers in England, in correspondence to Roger Conant himself in New England, Reverend John White was praising his efforts and urging him not to quit the colony. Sometime in the spring or summer of 1626, word finally reached the Cape Ann colonists that their employer, the Dorchester Company, had folded. Incredibly, the Dorchester Company had set aside funds to pay the back wages of its employees on Cape Ann and offered transportation back to England to any who wished to take it. According to William Hubbard, Reverend John White urged Conant to stay in New England with as many settlers as he could while White worked to establish a new company from the remnants of the Dorchester Company investors who still saw a potential for a profitable colony in the region and to obtain yet another new patent for the colony. Reverend John White even went so far as to hint that Roger Conant should relocate with those willing to stay to Naumkeag, which Conant had previously written White about as a more suitable location for a colony, and that he would work to obtain a patent for that colony.[109]

Many of the Cape Ann colonists chose to either return to England or try their hand at the slightly more established colonies of Virginia. Among those who abandoned Cape Ann for Virginia in 1626 was none other than Reverend Lyford, the man who had been the source of so much contention in the Plymouth Colony over the past few years. John Oldham decided to remain in the region to trade with the Natives of the area, but as he had turned down the Dorchester Company's offer to work as their trader, it is unlikely that it would have offered to pay for his transportation. At any rate, John Oldham was not one of the settlers who moved with Roger Conant to settle Naumkeag—and may have never even lived in Cape Ann at all—likely traveling and trading with various Native peoples throughout New England at this time. Of those who decided to remain with Roger Conant were William Allen, Thomas Gray, Richard Norman Sr., Richard Norman Jr., Peter Palfray, John Balch, Walter Knight, John Tylly and John Woodberry. These men, along with their families (whose names have been lost), chose for whatever reason to remain behind and try once again to build a new colony. In all, it is estimated that roughly twenty settlers remained behind to make the move to Naumkeag, and these settlers would become the first true inhabitants of what would in later years become Salem, Beverly and the Massachusetts Bay Colony.

It appears to be almost universally held by early New England historians (barring, of course, William Bradford, who characteristically makes no mention of the event) that the flight of so many of the Cape Ann Colony's settlers to England or Virginia was positive for the development of Massachusetts. Joseph Felt relates in *The Annals of Salem* that "the landsmen, except for a few of good character, embarked for home."[110] Clearly, Felt is implying that those who did not stay were decidedly *not* of "good character." Likewise, John Wingate Thorton writes that the offer of passage back to England or to Virginia by the Dorchester Company

> *was accepted by the ill-behaved, thriftless, or weak-minded portion, at once relieving the infant colony of the incubus of misrule and waste so depressing to all its interests. Thus happily freed from the drones and scum of their society, the colony, though greatly lessoned in numbers, yet really gained in strength, and now consisted only of the honest and industrious, who were resolved to remain faithful to the great object.*[111]

William Hubbard appears to hold a similar view of those who left, and the Reverend Thomas White definitely chastised them in the "Planter's Plea."

However, as much as those who chose to leave are labeled as "scum" or "drones" by the contemporary writers of that time and by so many later historians, it must be noted that none of these labels comes directly from Roger Conant or any of the other settlers remaining at Naumkeag. William Hubbard and Thomas White may have both heard such an opinion directly from Conant or any of the other settlers, but if that had happened, no direct quote is attributed. Rather, these statements come across as speculation on why this departure of so many may have indeed been a positive event for the colony. Certainly, there is no reference to an actual event or action by any of them that could be called "ill-behaved" or "waste." Of those who chose to depart, we have only the name of the Reverend John Lyford, and given what he had endured at the hands of the Plymouth authorities and the series of brutal winters, it's hardly surprising that he would be ready to quit New England altogether. As for the rest of those who chose to leave, it must be remembered that the first year of settling any new colony in North America was extremely difficult. Until 1625, only one colony in New England, the Plymouth Colony, had survived past one year, and it survived only after losing half of the population to famine and starvation. The earlier Popham Colony in Maine was abandoned after one year, and the Wessagussett Colony didn't last more than a few months into the winter and suffered an incredible loss of life. While there is probably no greater testament to Roger Conant's leadership than the survival of everyone in the Cape Ann Colony during the winter of 1625–26, that does not mean that this was an altogether pleasant experience. This becomes especially clear when one considers that the chief reason the Cape Ann Colony would need to be abandoned was that the colonists found that the soil was not suitable for growing crops. To survive that first winter, food would have been severely rationed. While shellfish, some shore fish and the occasional wild game would likely have been available and therefore able to stave off the worst starvation, vegetables, grains and fruits would have been severely lacking. The subsequent malnutrition and scurvy may well have been present among the settlers that winter.

Regardless of the difficulties faced by the settlers and the departure of so many of them, Roger Conant was determined to stay in Massachusetts and try to establish a colony at Naumkeag. William Hubbard, being a Puritan minister and thus prone to emphasize all things as being divinely inspired, describes Roger Conant at this time as something of a prophet:

> *Secretly conceiving in his mind, that in following times (as since has fallen out) it might prove a receptacle for such as upon the account of religion would be willing to begin a foreign plantation in this part of the world.*[112]

Hubbard added,

> *But Mr. Conant, as one inspired by some superior instinct, though never so earnestly pressed to go along with them, peremptorily declared his mind to wait the providence of God in that place where now they were, yea, though all the rest should forsake him, not doubting, as he said, but if they departed he should soon have more company....But that God who is ready to answer his people before they call, as he had filled the heart of that good man, Mr. Conant, in New England, with courage and resolution to abide fixed in his purpose, notwithstanding all opposition and persuasion he met with to the contrary, had also inclined the hearts of several others in Old England to be at work about the same design.*[113]

The Cape Ann colonists began the process of dismantling the clapboard house, fishing stages and any other structure they could to transport to their new home. By the early autumn of 1626, the colonists' few possessions were packed onto shallops for the short sail from Cape Ann to Naumkeag. In 1801, while digging for the foundation of a new home on March Street in Salem, a man uncovered the foundations of this first settlement, documented by the local minister of the East Church named Reverend William Bentley. The crude foundations were buried under about six feet of silt deposits, the result of massive erosion that took place throughout the region as a side effect of the deforestation brought on by the colonists in the seventeenth and eighteenth centuries. The foundations themselves weren't anything impressive, little more than fieldstone laid out in a roughly rectangular pattern.[114] However, this discovery did firmly establish that the first settlement at Salem (then called Naumkeag) occurred in the vicinity of Bridge Street, just south of where the modern Beverly Bridge stands today, facing the muddy North River rather than the more widely known historic areas along Derby and Essex Streets. Today, Roger Conant's old neighborhood lies beneath a railroad bridge, some power lines, a few residential homes and the onramp to the Beverly Bridge. The field, once known as Planter's Field, where these first settlers planted their first successful crops (the dire need for which forced them to abandon their first settlement at Cape Ann) now lies beneath a massive natural gas tank owned and operated by National Grid Utilities and the parking lot of Bill and Bob's Famous Roast Beef.

While the environment and landscape of this location has been completely transformed over the centuries, in 1626 this location was

March Street, Salem, Massachusetts, at sunset. This is the modern-day view of the North River from the site of the first settlement in Salem. *Photo by author.*

perfectly suited to the new colony's needs. The site lay just past the mouth where the North, Danvers and Bass Rivers meet, and while today these rivers are choked in mudflats at low tide, in 1626 (prior to deforestation) they were deep, clean and navigable. The low-lying strip of land along the North River would have been protected from the worst weather that the North Atlantic had to throw at them by a slight elevation in the landscape along where Bridge Street now runs. Given the silt deposits laid down over the centuries, the surrounding soil was fertile and could sustain several staple crops. In addition to this, the angle of the neck of land off Bridge Street along what is now called Collin's Cove (and was then named Shallop Cove) opposite of Salem Neck faced southeast and has ample sunlight and is often exposed to dry, salty winds coming in off Salem Sound, the perfect setting for drying codfish. While much of this area today bears little to remind us of those early days that Roger Conant and his party settled there, just across the harbor in Beverly lies a neighborhood still known as Fish Flake Hill, and the field around the National Grid Gas Tank is still known as Planter's Field. Planter's Field is a reference to the original

"Planters" of Naumkeag, and the name Fish Flake Hill refers to the fishing stages erected by Roger Conant and those early settlers when they moved to Beverly after the arrival of John Endicott and the Puritans in 1629.

These new settlers at Naumkeag, much like the Plymouth Colony a few years before them, did not enjoy the legal protection of any patent. It is unclear whether or not the colony would have a legal patent if the Dorchester Company had not folded, but either way, by relocating from Cape Ann to Naumkeag, they clearly were not under the jurisdiction of any previous patent. Reverend John White assured Roger Conant that there were still members of the Dorchester Company who, despite the incredible financial losses obtained by that company, still saw the opportunity to make a profit in that region if a settlement could be established and promised that if the settlers stayed he would obtain both a patent for and investment in the new colony. It would be another two years before Reverend John White was able to deliver on the promise, and when he finally did, it would come at the cost of Roger Conant's position as governor of the colony. While Roger Conant's official claim to that title would also likely have been lost along with the Dorchester Company that employed him, he certainly continued to both act and be perceived as such by the colonists during the intervening years of 1626–29.

Roger Conant may or may not have taken Reverend John White at his word that more investment, settlers and a patent would eventually come if they just held out at Naumkeag, but regardless, the more immediate needs

Pioneer Village, Salem, Massachusetts. Pioneer Village is a 1926 reconstruction of the type of homes that the early settlers to Salem may have built. *Photo by Ty Hapworth.*

of survival were pressing. It was, after all, the autumn of 1626; in a few short months, the harsh New England winter would be bearing down on them once again. They hadn't been able to plant the staple crops needed to sustain them through yet another cold and bitter winter. Naumkeag may have been the perfect location for planting the crops needed to sustain a colony, but the timing was anything but. Fortunately for the new settlers of Naumkeag, unlike Cape Ann, there were already people living there who, while not enjoying what could be considered an abundance of food, did at least have enough to help to sustain the small population of settlers that had recently arrived to their shores.

As discussed in previous chapters, this was a trying time for the Massachusett who lived around Naumkeag. Out of a population of thousands that had been reported by John Smith during his brief visit to the region in 1614, only a few dozen remained clustered in a few fortified villages that dotted the inlets and hills around what would later be called Salem Sound. Their sachem, Nanepashemet, had been killed by Tarrantine raids a few years earlier, and his wife, known only as Squaw Sachem, ruled over a once powerful and numerous people devastated by waves of diseases they had no knowledge of and cowed by incessant raids by hostile tribes to the north. Their enemies were armed with the latest in European firepower and sailing technology thanks to their trading relationships with the French and Basque. The recent hostilities that some of the tribe had initiated against the Plymouth Colony over the problems with the Wessagussett Colony had also ended in conflict with Europeans to the south and resulted in the destruction of a fortified village near what is now Ipswich, as well as the lives of several warriors they could ill-afford to lose at this time. Needless to say, the Massachusett found themselves in desperate need of new friends.

It is quite likely that the woman known as the "Squaw Sachem" and the Massachusett people she led were well aware of the animosity that existed between the Plymouth and Cape Ann Colonies, as they would have been watching their new neighbors closely and with a wary eye. It is equally as likely that Roger Conant had begun some type of dialogue with her prior to the settlers' removal to Naumkeag, as we know he had been looking into that area for some time as a more suitable location for a colony. Yet it must be acknowledged that this is purely speculation, as little was actually recorded by those colonists present at Cape Ann and Naumkeag during this time, and no information comes to us from the Massachusett. However, there is ample evidence that the Massachusett welcomed Roger Conant and the new settlers, as the two peoples quickly developed a mutually beneficial arrangement. William Dixy, a later settler that came to Salem in 1629 with John Endicott, recalled years later,

> *When we came to dwell heare, the Indians bid us welcome, and shewed*
> *themselves very glad that we came to dwell among them, and I understand*
> *that they had kindly entertained the English yt came hether before wee came,*
> *and the English and the Indians had a field in common, fenced in together,*
> *and the Indians fled to shelter themselves under the English oft times, saying*
> *they were afraid of theire enemy Indians in the contry: in particular, I*
> *remember sometime after we arrived, the Agawam Indians complained to*
> *Mr. Endecott that they were afraid of other Indians, called, as I take it,*
> *Tarrateens;—Hugh Browne was sent with others in a boate to Agawam*
> *for the Indians' reliefe, and, at other times, wee gave our neighbour Indians*
> *protection from their enemy Indians.*[115]

The passage asserts that, prior to Endecott's arrival, "the English and the Indians had a field in common." This is extremely telling of the relationship developed between the Massachuset and the settlers during that period between 1626 and 1629, when the only English present at Naumkeag were Roger Conant and the small band of settlers that had come over with him from Cape Ann. Clearly, some kind of arrangement and an understanding had been reached between the English and the Massachuset during those early years of settlement at Naumkeag. Such an arrangement, while clearly completely necessary to the very survival of both parties given the hardships both groups faced during that time and place, was also completely outside of the normal experience between colonists and Native Americans in North America during that time. The Plymouth Colony, while enjoying relatively decent relationships with their Wampanoag neighbors, never "had a field in common" with them, let alone offered shelter and protection from raiding rival tribes. On the contrary, the Plymouth Colony even quickly fortified its settlement as protection from the threat of a Native attack. The Popham Colony in Maine lived in constant fear of the sour relationships with the local tribes during their brief stay there in 1607, and the Wessagussett Colony had a clearly disastrous relationship with the Massachuset, the very people who now so firmly allied themselves to the English settlers at Naumkeag. Even far to the south in Virginia, relations with the Native tribes were anything but peaceful, and the 1620s were marred by incredible violence between settlers and Native Americans. Only at Naumkeag, and later briefly at another settlement in Massachusetts known as Merrymont, do we see a genuinely positive and mutually beneficial relationship between the English and the Native Americans in North America during this decade. While it is true that this arrangement was forged out of mutual necessity, it must also be noted that issues facing the English and the Massachusett at Naumkeag were not entirely unique from the issues facing other groups of colonists and Native Americans. Other English colonies faced starvation and famine during their early years, and clearly other Native peoples faced violent conflict with rival Natives. Yet only at Naumkeag at this stage do we see the two groups living so closely aligned, sharing each other's fields, crops and even homes in times of need. Regrettably, this period of tranquility between the English and the Massachusett would prove to be short-lived.

8

BECOMING SALEM

*The Arrival of John Endecott, Conflict, Compromise
and the Establishment of a Government*

O n June 20, 1628, the ship *Abigail* under the command of Captain
Henry Gauden set sail from Weymouth, England. Unbeknownst
to Roger Conant and the settlers at Naumkeag, onboard the *Abigail*
was the new governor of the fledgling colony, John Endecott, along with
his wife, Jane Francis Endecott. Other passengers included Charles Gott,
Richard and William Brakenberry, Richard Davenport, Hugh Laskin,
Lawrence Leach, Roger Morey, John Elford, Thomas Puckett, Samuel
and John Browne and a few dozen other settlers whose names have been
lost to history (including the wives and families of Charles Gott and Hugh
Laskin).[116] John Woodbury, who had returned to England the previous year
to plead the case for the continuation of the Cape Ann Colony at Naumkeag
for Roger Conant and the original settlers, was also on board along with his
son Humphrey.

It is likely that John Woodbury had returned to England with the ill-
fated fishing vessel that had left the Cape Ann Colony in 1626 loaded with
salt cod and optimism for a solid return on the Dorchester Company's
investment, only instead to find economic ruin for the company when war
broke out between England and both France and Spain and the English cod
market became glutted as a result. Yet regardless of how John Woodbury
took passage back to England, he soon found himself united in an alliance
with the Reverend John White in an effort to secure some kind of financial
backing for the abandoned colony now at Naumkeag.

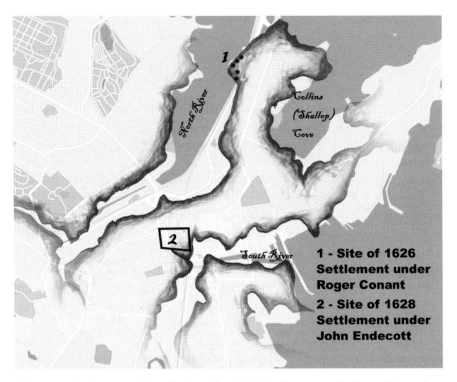

1 - Site of 1626 Settlement under Roger Conant
2 - Site of 1628 Settlement under John Endecott

Salem map showing approximately where the original settlements under Roger Conant in 1626 and John Endecott in 1628 in relation to the historic coastline and modern coastline and city streets. *Map by Justin Patterson.*

While the settlement of the Cape Ann Colony had been a complete financial disaster for the investors of the Dorchester Company, the settlers under Roger Conant had been able to achieve something that no previous English North American settlement had been able to achieve up until that time: they had survived multiple winters without a single loss of life. After all, both Plymouth and Jamestown had suffered appalling casualties their first few years, the Popham Colony and the Roanoke Colony had both ceased to exist after less than a year and the Wessagussett Colony under Thomas Weston had completely collapsed in just a few short months. In a world where the simple act of surviving was considered a remarkable achievement, the Cape Ann Colony had been a resounding success, even if it was a complete and utter financial failure. It also must be noted that while the Cape Ann Colony was a financial failure, Roger Conant and the rest of the colonists now at Naumkeag could hardly bear any of the responsibility for that. They had succeeded in catching fish, salting fish and packing a ship full of fish to sell in the markets of Europe. The financial failure of that expedition had far more to do with the incessant military rivalry between England and its European adversaries than it did to any lack of effort or ability on the colonists' part. Even the abandonment of Cape Ann for Naumkeag can hardly be seen as anything other than a wise course of action following the discovery that Cape Ann was simply unsuited for any kind of substantial agriculture. Yet while Roger Conant had been remarkably successful in his efforts given the circumstances, the fact remained that Naumkeag Colony was only squatting on land that it had no legal claim to and had no financial backing on which to rely on back home. To make matters worse, confidence in his leadership was intentionally being undermined in England by accusations of the settlers of the Cape Ann Colony as being "ill-chosen and commanded." Securing legal title and further financial backing for the colony was far from guaranteed.

Fortunately for the efforts of John Woodbury, Reverend John White was still one of the most influential men involved in the Dorchester Company, and he wasn't ready to abandon the project simply because the colony had failed to turn a profit. With Charles I as king, the future for Puritans in England was looking rather grim, and many Puritans were eager to establish a colony with some degree of self-governance far removed from the eyes of the king. For Reverend John White, financial concerns were secondary to ecclesiastical and nationalistic ones, and he saw great potential for any colony that could survive in Massachusetts. By 1627, Reverend John White had gathered together several of the former investors of the Dorchester Company to form the new Massachusetts Bay Company. Among the initial investors in the Massachusetts Bay Company were Sir Henry Roswell, Sir John Young, Thomas Southcoat, John Humphrey, Simon Whitcomb and John Endecott. Soon the cousin of John Endecott's wife, Jane, Matthew Craddock, would also join the Massachusetts Bay Company. In time, Craddock would become the chief financial backer of the company and serve as co-governor of the colony with John Endecott. Rather than use the existing and questionable patent the Dorchester Company under Lord Sheffield obtained from the Council of New England, the new Massachusetts Bay Company decided instead to petition King Charles I directly for a patent to settle in New England.[117] Once again, conflicting patents would cause a great deal of trouble for those who were settling in Massachusetts. Unfortunately, like so many other legal documents and correspondence pertaining to the early settlement of Salem, this patent has also been lost.

The co-governorship arrangement of the Massachusetts Bay Colony seems to have worked remarkably well. Under this arrangement, it was agreed that John Endicott would serve as the governor of the colony in Massachusetts while Matthew Craddock would serve as the governor of the colony in England and oversee the company's efforts there. Why the Reverend John White chose Matthew Craddock and John Endicott as governors of the colony rather than continue to support Roger Conant, whom he had originally supported, is a mystery. However, given the massive capital brought to the project by Matthew Craddock, we can certainly speculate that this may well have been a simple case of nepotism. After all, John Endicott was one of the first investors to sign on to the new Massachusetts Bay Colony, and it is entirely possible that his offer to bring his wealthy cousin and all the capital needed for this enterprise was conditioned on their being appointed as governors of the colony. We can never know for certain what Reverend John White's motivations were, but records show that over half of the costs of John Endicott's initial voyage to Massachusetts were paid out of the pocket of Matthew Craddock.[118] It is also around this time that Reverend John White began to disparage the leadership of Roger Conant at the Cape Ann Colony. While summarizing the previous attempts to settle Massachusetts in 1630, the Reverend John White wrote,

> *Unto these losses by fishing, were added two other no small disadvantages; the one in the country by our land-men, who being ill chosen and ill commanded, fell into many disorders, and did the Company little service; the other by the fall of the price of shipping, which was now abated to more than the one half; by which means it came to pass, that our ships, which stood us in little less than £1200, were sold for £480.*[119]

The reverend later added,

> *But a few of the most honest and industrious resolved to stay behind, and to take charge of the cattle sent over the year before; which they performed accordingly. And not liking their seat at Cape Anne, chosen especially for the supposed commodity of fishing, they transported themselves to Nahum-Keike (meaning Naumkeag, or Salem), about four or five leagues distant to the south-west from Cape Anne.*[120]

It's quite obvious that in both of these passages, Reverend John White is referring to Roger Conant. How can the leadership of the Cape Ann Colony under Roger Conant be both described as "the most honest and industrious" *and* as "ill chosen and ill commanded" by the same person?

White was the individual who had originally tapped Roger Conant to lead the Dorchester Company's operations on Cape Ann to begin with. Just like the failure of William Bradford before him, Reverend John White's refusal to name Roger Conant in any leadership capacity during this time seems to speak volumes about what his motivation may have been. It is apparent that Reverend John White was cognizant of the narrative that was unfolding about the settlement of the Cape Ann/Naumkeag Colony. Like John Smith and William Bradford before him, he wrote his descriptions of the colony and New England as part of an effort to induce more financial investment and immigration. Thus, his writings, while likely somewhat accurate, must be viewed critically. It seems that Reverend John White was trying to tread a fine line between both establishing a solid argument for John Endecott to take over the leadership of the now Massachusetts Bay Colony while also extolling the virtues of the very people whose authority John Endecott was about to usurp.

Regardless of the reasons behind the efforts of Reverend John White to push Roger Conant out of both his role as governor as well as his place in the founding narrative of the colony, the simple fact was that when *Abigail* arrived in Naumkeag on September 6, 1628, the ship brought a new governor with a new vision for how the colony was to be managed. Unfortunately, it appears that all of the original documentation regarding the landing of John Endecott at Naumkeag has been lost to history. It is unknown how many settlers Endicott brought with him, though several scholars estimate that the exact number was somewhere between 80 and 150 people. There isn't even any certainty about where exactly in Salem the *Abigail* landed. Most historians seem to think that it was likely near where Front Street in Salem sits today. At the time, that bit of land was shoreline, and soon after Endicott's landing, homes were constructed in that area. However, it is just as likely that the *Abigail* first landed near Roger Conant's original settlement on what is now Bridge Street Neck along the North River. Yet while any documentation surrounding Endecott's orders from the Massachusetts Bay Company or any narrative written about this momentous event in American history has been lost, a great deal about this encounter can be gleaned from responses to letters written by John Endecott to his co-governor Matthew Craddock and to the Massachusetts Bay Colony. These missives were written the following year and have thankfully been preserved. On April 17, 1629, the Massachusetts Bay Company wrote a "Letter of General Instructions to Endicott and his Council":

And that it may appear, as well to all the world, as to the old planters themselves, that we seek not to make them slaves, (as it seems by your letter some of them think themselves to become by means of our Patent), we are content they shall be partakers of such privileges as we, from his Majesty's especial grace, with great cost, favor of personages of note, and much labor, have obtained; and that they shall be incorporated into this Society, and enjoy not only those lands which formerly they have manured, but such a further proportion as by the advice and judgment of yourself, and the rest of the Council, shall be thought fit for them, or any of them. And besides, it is still our purpose that they should have some benefit by the common stock, as was by your first commission directed and appointed with this addition, that if it be held too much to take thirty per cent, and the freight of the goods for and in consideration of our adventure and disbursement of our moneys, to be paid in beaver at six shillings per pound, that you moderate the said rate, as you with the rest of the Council shall think to be agreeable to equity and good conscience.

And our further orders is, that none be partakers of any the aforesaid privileges and profits, but such as be peaceable men, and of honest life and conversation, and desirous to live amongst us, and conform themselves to good order and government. And as touching the old planters, their earnest desire for the present to continue the planting of tobacco, (a trade by this whole Company generally disavowed, and utterly disclaimed by some of the greatest adventurers amongst us, who absolutely declared themselves unwilling to have any hand in this Plantation if we intended to cherish or permit the planting thereof, or any other kind, than for a man's private use, for mere necessity,) we are of opinion the old planters will have small encouragement to that employment; for we find here, by late experience, that it doth hardly produce the freight and custom; neither is there hope of amendment, there being such great quantities made in other places, that ere long it is like to be little worth. Nevertheless, if the old planters, (for we exclude all others,) conceive that they cannot otherwise provide for their livelihood, we leave it to the discretion of yourself and the Council there, to give way for the chap. present to their planting of it in such manner and with such restrictions as you and the said Council shall think fitting; having an especial care, with as much conveniency as may be, utterly to suppress the planting of it, except for mere necessity. But, however, we absolutely forbid the sale of it, or the use of it, by any of our own or particular men's servants, unless upon urgent occasion, for the benefit of health, and taken privately.[121]

While this response was dated April 17, 1629, the letter indicates that it was written as a response to a letter written by Endicott on September 13, 1628, only one week after the landing of the *Abigail* at Naumkeag. Obviously, conflict between the "Old Planters" under Roger Conant and the "New Planters" under John Endecott began the moment the *Abigail* dropped anchor. It appears that the Old Planters were rather untrusting of their new neighbors, and with good reason. It would be a gross understatement to say that the relationship between the founders of the earlier Cape Ann Colony and the religious authorities governing the Plymouth Colony were less than ideal. Those in command of this new expedition shared far more in common with the religious leadership of Plymouth than they did with the more pragmatic fishing interests that had made up the majority of the previous benefactors of the Cape Ann Colony. While the frustrating experiences the Old Planters had with the Plymouth Colony clearly made them more than a little prejudiced toward their new neighbors, the most telling line in the Massachusetts Bay Colony's letter to Endicott is this one: "And that it may appear, as well to all the world, as to the old planters themselves, that we seek not to make them slaves, (as it seems by your letter some of them think themselves to be become by means of our Patent)." Throughout the rest of the letters written by both Matthew Craddock and the Massachusetts Bay Company, as well as receipts and invoices, are references to "servants" of either individuals or of the company itself. These servants were people who had signed letters of indenture with an employer to provide essentially free labor with few rights in exchange for transportation, food and lodging for a set period of time (usually seven years). Much of the skilled and unskilled labor that would be needed to establish the colony and make it profitable was to be performed by such indentured servants. As governor, John Endecott was granted a great deal of authority over the lives of these servants, as indicated by the instructions he received from the Massachusetts Bay Company in the same April 17 letter:

> *For the better accommodation of businesses, we have divided the servants belonging to the Company into several families, as we desire and intend they should live together; a copy whereof we send you here enclosed, that you may accordingly appoint each man his charge and duty. Yet it is not our intent to tie you so strictly to this direction, but that in your discretion, as you shall see cause from time to time, you may alter or displace any as you shall think fit.*

Our earnest desire is that you take special care, in settling these families, that the chief in the family, at least some of them, be grounded in religion; whereby morning and evening family duties may be duly performed, and a watchful eye held over all in each family, by one or more in each family to be appointed thereto, that so disorders may be prevented, and weeds nipped before they take too great a head. It will be a business worthy your best endeavors to look unto this in the beginning, and, if need be, to make some exemplary to all the rest otherwise your government will be esteemed as a scarecrow. Our desire is to use lenity, all that may be; but, in case of necessity, not to neglect the other, knowing that correction is ordained for the fool's back. And as we intend not to be wanting on our parts to provide all things needful for the maintenance and sustenance of our servants, so may we justly, by the laws of God and man, require obedience and honest carriage from them, with fitting labor in their several employments; wherein if they shall be wanting, and much more if refractory, care must be taken to punish the obstinate and disobedient, being as necessary as food and raiment. And we heartily pray you, that all be kept to labor, as the only means to reduce them to civil, yea a godly life, and to keep youth from falling into many enormities, which by nature we are all too much inclined unto. God, who alone is able and powerful, enable you to this great work, and grant that our chiefest aim may be his honor and glory. And thus wishing you all happy and prosperous success.[122]

As these instructions state clearly, the new governor would wield considerable control and influence over the lives of those classified as "servants" in the new colony. Everything from where they could settle, who the head of their households would be, the type of work they would perform and how they were expected to worship was all given over to Governor John Endicott's discretion. Given the wording of these instruction, the concern that the Massachusetts Bay Company sought to "make them [the Old Planters] slaves" was not simply hyperbole. These new "servants" shared quite a lot in common with the Old Planters. Both groups were drawn primarily from the poor and working classes of England, both groups were heavily made up of skilled laborers, and arguably most importantly, both groups contained many adherents to the traditional practices of the Church of England rather than the practices favored by the Puritan leadership of the Massachusetts Bay Company. Many of the Old Planters under Roger Conant had similarly been employed as servants for the Dorchester Company at Cape Ann. It is not at all unreasonable that the Old Planters would have serious misgivings about their new neighbors. After all, John Endicott also brought with him the news that Roger Conant was no longer governor and that any claim that they may have had to the land they had settled at Naumkeag was now null and void given the new patent that had been obtained from King Charles I.

The Old Planters' anxieties over their new neighbors could not have been eased when Governor John Endicott took possession of the frame house that had previously been the home of Roger Conant. Governor Endicott had the home disassembled and reused the materials to build his own new governor's mansion near where the corner of Church and Washington Streets is in Salem today.[123] Governor Endicott also established new laws governing the morality of the settlers at Naumkeag, such as the prohibition against the cultivation and sale of tobacco. As is apparent in the Massachusetts Bay Company's letter of instructions to Governor Endicott, the company approved of Endecott's efforts to placate the Old Planters' fears by allowing them to continue to cultivate tobacco so long as they did not trade with any of the new arrivals or any indentured servants employed by them. In addition to these allowances, the Massachusetts Bay Company also, after some urging by Conant through Endecott, granted all the Old Planters the same rights and privileges enjoyed by stockholders of the company in recognition of their work in establishing the colony.[124]

Despite these efforts to reach a common understanding between these two camps, it appears that many of the Old Planters continued to have strained relationships with the New Planters for many years to come. A few of the Old Planters would find themselves in serious legal trouble. Thomas Gray was fined and publicly flogged for drunkenness, and in 1630, John Pickryn was confined to the stocks for being the accessory to some unnamed felony. Others would find themselves the victim of rumor and gossip. For example, it was said of Walter Knight that he "lived with his wife more before than after the wedding."[125] Not all of the Old Planters fared poorly with the New Planters—William Trask would even serve as John Endecott's color-bearer—but it does seem that friction remained in the colony between the two camps for many years. Before long, the Old Planters left their homes on the banks of the North River to move to the "Cape Ann Side of Salem" (modern Beverly, Massachusetts), to put more distance between themselves and the newcomers. Later in his life, Roger Conant related to the Massachusetts General Court that the people of Salem had taken to mocking them by calling Beverly "Beggardly."[126] It may be that the move from the North River to Beverly had been part of the agreement reached to ease the tensions between the New and Old Planters, but that is pure speculation. Still, snide remarks and the occasional legal infraction aside, the political leadership of the colony had changed hands with the consent of Roger Conant, with due acknowledgement given to the contributions of the Old Planters in finding and establishing the new colony and without any legal challenges or bloodshed.

In May 1629, Governor Endecott received another communication from his cousin and co-governor in England Matthew Craddock that provided further guidance over establishing a government over the new Massachusetts Bay Colony at Naumkeag. The "Act of Court" over "the Governor and Council of London's Plantation in the Massachusetts Bay in New England" authorized Governor Endicott to appoint members to a local council and hold elections for governor, deputy governor, secretary and whatever other officers may be required. This council and these officers were charged with establishing the laws of the new colony, calling courts to investigate and judge on infractions to those laws and enforcing those laws. Interestingly, the Act of Court also required the person serving as governor to vote with the majority of the council so as to ensure the validity of any law or ruling the council passed. This is very likely the first example of a check of power on an executive body by a legislative body, a foundational principal of the United States Constitution, in American history. An oath was sent over along with the Act of Court to be administered to John Endecott and the officers and council members, thus establishing the first real governmental body of Massachusetts.[127] In order to ensure that the Old Planters accepted the new regime, two seats on this council were reserved for them. While the minutes and other records of this first Massachusetts council have been lost to history, a derisive comment by Thomas Morton that one of the Old Planters appointed to the council was a "cowherder" seems to indicate that John Woodbury was one of them. Given his former position as governor and his later involvement in various civic functions around Salem and Beverly for the remainder of his life, it is highly likely that Roger Conant was the other.

There is no record of what the Massachusett and the woman known as Squaw Sachem who led them made of these developments. While they were certainly present during the arrival of Endecott's party, no chronicler records any mention of their involvement or even presence during this time. This is most likely because of the fact that since there were Englishmen already living at the site and the Massachsett were led by a woman, the new party of Englishmen felt no need to consult with or make provisions for anyone other than their fellow countrymen in order to establish themselves there. While Puritan attitudes toward First Nations' claims to the land of

New England would dramatically change over the next few years from indifference to eager engagement, at this moment it does not appear that any consideration was given. As the reign of Charles I became more and more antagonistic toward the Puritans and Parliament (and would erupt into all-out civil war by the 1640s), New England Puritans would go to great lengths to actually purchase title to their lands directly from First Nation leaders. The reason for this change in attitude was that the Puritans recognized the need to be able to legally argue to a right to their settlements completely independent of a grant from the king under English law, regardless of the fact that Massachusett concepts and understandings of property ownership were completely different than that of the English. This practice continued throughout the seventeenth century long after the execution of Charles I, the reign of Oliver Cromwell and the restoration of the monarchy. However, no deed was acquired for Salem from any First Nation peoples until 1686, several decades after the settlement of Salem took place. Clearly, the opinions of the Massachusett at this time were of little significance to the new arrivals, and if anything of their opinion was recorded, it has been long since lost.

It is also at this time that we first start to see the name Salem appear in various records. While it is uncertain exactly when the settlement at Naumkeag became Salem, it seems that it was around the time of Endecott's arrival that the name Salem began to be used interchangeably with Naumkeag. When Reverend Francis Higginson arrived in 1629, he referred to Salem as both "Nahumkek" and "Salem" in the same account of his voyage and settlement.[128] According to the "Planter's Plea," the name Salem was bestowed on the settlement in honor of the accommodation reached between the Old Planters and the New Planters. The Planter's Plea also seems to indicate that Nahumkek may have been an intentional mispronunciation of Naumkeag, as it seems that some religiously minded Puritans felt that Naumkeag sounded an awful lot like the Hebrew phrase for "bosom of consolation," *Nahum Keike*. The full relevant passage of the "Planter's Plea" reads as follows:

> *Howsoever it bee, it fals out that the name of the place, which our late Colony hath chosen for their seat, prooves to bee perfect Hebrew, being called Nahum Keike, by interpretation, The bosome of consolation: which it were pitty that those which observed it not, should change into the name of Salem, though upon a faire ground, in remembrance of a peace setled upon a conference at a generall meeting betweene them and their neighbours, after expectance of some dangerous jarred.*

However, according to William Hubbard, the name was bestowed on the settlement with the arrival of a Reverend Higginson in 1629 for the purposes of giving the city a more Christian name. Salem would officially be recognized as Salem under the new charter it received in 1629, but that also appears to be an acknowledgement of the name that was already in use. It is most likely that the name Salem was both an honor of the accommodation reached between the Old and New Planters *and* a way of placing thoroughly Christian stamp on the young colony. Clearly by choosing to change the name of the settlement from Naumkeag to Salem, the Puritans were intending to send a message to their contemporaries about the kind of city that they were founding. Salem is the Latinization of a word of Hebrew origin that means "peace" and is associated with the Hebrew Shalom, the Arabic Salaam and the city of Jerusalem. Thus the "good fishing place" for the Algonquin, Naumkeag (or Nahumkek), settled by a motley crew of West Country fishermen and their families, became the "City of Peace" for the hundreds of Puritan immigrants that would soon arrive on Salem's shores to settle the Massachusetts Bay Colony. The name Salem then appears to have been chosen both as a testament to the peaceful resolution to various potentially violent conflicts in the years leading up to and including the arrival of the New Planters under Endecott and as a thoroughly Protestant Christian stamp on the founding city of the new Puritan-dominated Massachusetts Bay Colony. Roger Conant and the "Old Planters" who settled Naumkeag after abandoning the Cape Ann Colony were, in the eyes of the Puritan contemporaries, being moved by the hand of God to create a foundation for the Puritans to build their New England, just as the European diseases that had decimated the Native inhabitants living there before them were the work of God. Clearly, this Naumkeag—with its lack of bloodshed and lack of death— was the exception in the establishment of new colonies in North America. This beautiful place with an abundance of fish, where their countrymen lived in apparent harmony with the Natives of the land and where conflict with their neighboring colony of Plymouth was resolved through reason instead of strife, was a place of peace. Clearly, this was their Salem.

9

THE FIRST HALF CENTURY

1628–1679

John Endecott's brief tenure as governor of the Massachusetts Bay Colony was a trying time for the colony. Almost immediately, the Plymouth Colony requested assistance in chastising another rogue colony recently established near present-day Mount Wollaston in Quincy, Massachusetts, by a man named Captain Wollaston. According to William Bradford, while Captain Wollaston was away, one of his men, Thomas Morton, declared himself to be

> *the Lord of Misrule, and maintained (as it were) a school of atheism. And after they had got some goods into their hands, and got much by trading with the Indians, they spent it vainly quaffing and drinking, both wine and strong waters in great excess....They also set up a maypole, inviting the Indian women for their consorts, dancing and frisking together like so many fairies or furies, rather, and worse practices.*[129]

William Bradford also accused Thomas Morton of writing erotic poetry. The Plymouth Colony was concerned that the Native Americans frolicking with Morton might get access to firearms and that the existence of such a colony would entice their own indentured servants to flee to the interior. It is against this backdrop that Plymouth sent word to the new Salem Colony and to the fishing post at Piscataqua (Portsmouth, New Hampshire) to request assistance in chastising the colony at Mount Wollaston that was becoming known as "Merrymount." John Endecott quickly agreed to lend aid, and a detachment of Salem Puritans joined the Pilgrims under Myles

Standish in destroying the colony. John Endecott himself chopped down the maypole and ordered Thomas Morton to be flogged. Endecott's actions at Merrymount would later be fictionalized in the short story "The Maypole of Merrymount" by Salem's favorite son and author Nathaniel Hawthorne.

By the winter of 1628–29, approximately two hundred people (give or take a few dozen) were living at Salem. The two dozen or so Old Planters under Conant were either still along Bridge Street Neck or had already moved across the river to the "Cape Ann Side" or "Bass River Side" of Salem that would later become Beverly. The remaining settlers established themselves in the vicinity of Essex and Washington Streets, where a small palisaded fort was built. The walls of that fort followed the modern block formed by Washington, Essex, Crombie, and Norman Streets.[130] At that time, the area now encompassing Derby Street and Riley Plaza was taken up by a wide and deep bend in the South River, so ships could have sailed right up to unload cargo and settlers near where the intersection of New Derby Street, Washington and Norman Streets lies today. A few scattered buildings were constructed outside the palisade, including John Endecott's reconstructed governor's home, but most of the settlers lived, worked and died within that small city block—and died they did.

The first deaths that occurred in the history of the Cape Ann/Naumkeag/ Salem Colony occurred that first winter of John Endecott's governorship. Like many ill-fated colonial endeavors before him, the New Planters had arrived far too late in the season to adequately prepare for winter, and soon famine set in. With no doctor among them, Salem requested assistance from Plymouth, which sent Dr. Fuller to do what he could for the starving colony. John Endecott's wife, Jane Francis, was one of the first to die, and soon several more followed. While there is no exact record of the number of Salem colonists who died during the winter of 1628–29 (just as there is no exact record for the number colonists who were living there), that winter must have been brutal. Before it was over, John Endecott took the extreme measure of casting all of the indentured servants out of the colony and into the wilderness to fend for themselves.[131]

Despite the hardship of the winter of 1628–29, the colony did survive. In April 1629, John Endecott was reelected as governor, and in the summer of 1629, a new wave of a few hundred settlers arrived from England and brought with them the first new ministers of Salem, Reverend Higginson and Reverend Skelton, who established First Church in Salem, which still remains as the oldest Protestant congregation in America and is a Unitarian Universalist Congregation in the Christian tradition today. That summer,

John Endecott also dispatched a party under a recent arrival named Thomas Graves to lay claim to what would become Charlestown, Massachusetts. The winter of 1629–30 also proved to be a difficult one, though not as horrific as the previous winter. In June 1630, the famous Winthrop Fleet of eleven ships and nearly one thousand new settlers arrived in Salem before quickly removing to establish Boston. The Great Puritan Migration had begun.

With the Puritans came thousands of laborers, indentured servants and, later, some enslaved Africans. As the population expanded, more and more fishermen began to settle permanently in New England. Indeed, by 1642, Gloucester was firmly established on the same site that Roger Conant had to abandon on Cape Ann in 1626. It was settled by West Country fishermen who could be supported through trade with the numerous Puritan farms that dotted coastal New England. Likewise, fishing communities sprang up throughout Cape Cod, Maine, New Hampshire and the North Shore. These fishing communities would lay the foundation for the great maritime economy of fishing, whaling, shipbuilding and trade that would make New England such an economic powerhouse for the British Empire and later the United States of America. Given the nature of this work, skilled trades that required large groups of diverse people to coordinate their efforts either as sailors on a ship or in the construction of a ship, it is no surprise that New England would emerge as the birthplace of both American democracy and the Industrial Revolution.

While religion may be the stamp that religious writers and authorities wove through their narratives and in their letters, and indeed was the cause of both much conflict and conflict resolution during this time, the real powerhouse that fueled the settlement of the Americas by Europeans was economics. Nowhere is this more apparent than in New England, the very land most associated with religious extremism during this time. Fish—namely, dried and salted cod—was then (and to a lesser extent remains so today) an extraordinarily valuable commodity and for well over one hundred years prior to the settlement of New England was the resource that Europeans sought to exploit for their own economic gain. Indeed, even to this day, the Massachusetts State House sports the "Sacred Cod," a wooden effigy of a codfish that hangs in the house chamber as a testament to the fish whose existence was so vital to the development of Massachusetts.

Around 1631, the theologian and future founder of Rhode Island Roger Williams came to Salem. In his work *Twice Told Tales*, Nathaniel Hawthorne recalls an incident where after some urging from Roger Williams to destroy all idolatrous symbols, John Endecott removed the Cross of Saint George from the flag of New England with the cut of a saber while an Old Planter clasped in the stocks accuses him of treason. How true the tale of "Endecott and the Cross" actually was is open to some speculation, but it is around this time that the Cross of Saint George is replaced by the more secular pine tree in the flag of New England.

In August 1632, another Tarrantine raid destroyed the Massachusett settlement of Agawam on Cape Ann, further cementing the Massachusetts Bay Colony's alliance with the Massachusett and lead the colony to establish a blockhouse there to protect the region from future raids.[132] Sadly, the Plymouth Colony's relationships with its Native American neighbors would continue to sour. By 1636, tensions between the different First Nations peoples of New England and the Plymouth Colony would lead to the death of John Oldham on Block Island at the hands of the Narragansett People of Rhode Island, who were angry that he was trading with the Pequot of Connecticut. Plymouth then chose to back the Narragansett in their claim of trading rights over the Pequot, which then led to the Pequot War. The English colonies of Massachusetts Bay, Rhode Island and Connecticut would be dragged into that conflict on the side of Plymouth and the Narragansetts, and this would result in the first intentional act of genocide in New England's history: the Pequot Nation was nearly extinguished at the hands of English and Narragansett forces, with the survivors sold into slavery (though some Pequot survived and their descendants remain in Connecticut and Wisconsin today). While there is no record of Roger Conant ever participating in any violent acts or military expeditions against any of the Native peoples of the region, it is not at all certain that he did not participate in the Pequot War.

After his time as governor, Roger Conant remained active in the civic life of Salem, Beverly and the growing Commonwealth of Massachusetts. In 1631, he finally officially became a "freeman"—meaning someone who could vote and hold office—in the colony he had founded five years earlier and attended his first session of the Massachusetts General Court in Boston. In 1634, he was elected as one of Salem's representatives to the Massachusetts General Court. As a representative to the General Court, he was involved with a heated disagreement between Governor John Winthrop and the Massachusetts General Court over whether or not the court had the right to set budgets and debate and make laws or simply assent to the budget presented by the governor and rule on the legality of questions to the law. The General Court prevailed in this debate, and the compromise reached with Governor Winthrop would lay the foundation for the relationship between the Massachusetts legislature and the Governor's Office in future

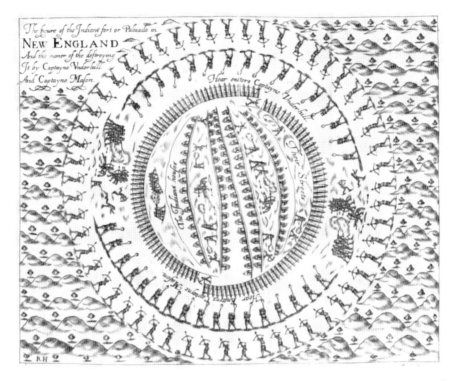

Attack on a Pequot village by English and Narragansett forces, from a 1638 print. *Courtesy of the New York Public Library.*

generations.[133] However, Conant's time with the Massachusetts Court was short-lived, and soon he chose to focus his attention closer to home. In 1659, he led an effort to petition the Massachusetts General Court to allow for the Bass River side of Salem to break away and form a new settlement, which finally became Beverly in 1668. Sadly, 1668 was also the year Sarah Conant died. The Conant family were active members of both First Church in Salem and then later helped found First Parish in Beverly after that town split from Salem. Roger Conant surveyed the first road to what later became Manchester by the Sea (still the most scenic drive on the North Shore) and was involved in a brief but ultimately futile effort to try and bring Harvard University to Salem. Roger Conant's work can be clearly seen in the establishment of the government of Massachusetts and several early local municipalities despite incredible efforts on the part of some of his contemporaries to write both him and the working people he led out of the history altogether.

It therefore seems fitting that we should let Roger Conant speak for himself as we close this book. Toward the end of his life, he petitioned the General

Court of Massachusetts on behalf of himself, his family and the families of those who had first migrated with him from Cape Ann to Naumkeag for greater recognition of the role they played in the founding of the colony. He also wanted to change the name of Beverly because he didn't like that the people of Salem had taken to calling it "Beggarly" and to make it clear he had nothing to do with changing the name of Naumkeag to Salem. In this document from 1671, at the age of seventy-nine, Roger Conant wrote what is possibly the only firsthand narrative about those early years of settlement at Naumkeag:

> *The umble peticion of Roger Conant of Basriver, alias Beverly, who have bin a planter in New England fortie eight yeers and upward, being one of the first, if not the first, that resolved and made good my settlement under God…and have bin instrumentall, both for the founding and carrying on the same, and when in the infancy thereof, it was in danger of being deserted, I was a means through grace assisting me, to stop the flight of those few that were then here with me, and that by my utter denial to go away with them, would have gon either for England or mostly for Virginia, but thereupon stayed to the hassard of our lives. Now my umble sute and request is unto this honorable Court onlie that the name of our town or plantation may be altered or changed from Beverly and be called Budleigh, I have two reasons that have moved me unto this request. The first is the great dislike and discontent of many of our people for this name of Beverly, because (wee being but a small place) it hath caused on us a Constant nickname of beggarly.…Secondly. I being the first that had house in Salem (and never had any hand in naming either that or any other towne) and myself with those that were then with me, being all from the western part of England, desire this western name of Budleigh…where myself was borne.…I never made suite or request unto the Generall Court for the least matter, tho' I thinke I might as well have done, as many others have, who have obtained much without the hassard of life or preferring the publick good before theire own interest, which, I praise God, I have done.*[134]

The General Court of Massachusetts rejected this plea, the one time Conant ever asked them for anything after all the incredible work he and his followers from Cape Ann had done to secure a foothold for that colony on the shores of what would come to be called Salem Sound. Roger Conant passed away quietly in his sleep eight years later at his home in Budleigh, Massachusetts, in 1679.

NOTES

1. The New England That Was

1. John Wingate Thornton, *The Landing at Cape Ann; or the Charter of the First Permanent Colony on the Territory of the Massachusetts Company* (British Library, 1854), 1.
2. William Cronan, *Changes in the Land: Indians, Colonists, and the Ecology of New England* (New York: Hill & Wang, 1983), 26.
3. Marshall H. Saville, *Champlain and His Landings at Cape Ann, 1605, 1606* (Rockport, MA: Sandy Bay Historical Society, 1930), 458–60.
4. Ibid., 463–65.
5. John Smith, *A Description of New England* (Humphry Lowenes at London, 1616), 37–38.
6. Ibid., 37.
7. Sidney Perley, *History of Salem* (Salem, MA: S. Perley, 1924), 31.
8. Ibid., 29–31.
9. Ronald Dale Karr, *Indian New England, 1524–1674* (Pepperell, MA: Branch Line Press, 1999), 140–41.
10. Ibid., 140.
11. Perley, *History of Salem*, 27–28.
12. William Hubbard, *A General History of New England* (Boston: Charles C. Little and James Brown, 1848), 31.
13. Ibid., 30.
14. H.M., *Echoes of the Mystic Side: Malden, Melrose, Everett* (Boston: Educational Publishing Company 1890), 9.
15. Thornton, *Landing at Cape Ann*, 52.

2. The Fishermen

16. Clifford Shipton, *Roger Conant: A Founder of Massachusetts* (Cambridge, MA: Harvard University Press, 19440, 51.

17. Ibid., 53.

18. Mary Hervey, *The Life and Correspondence of Thomas Howard, Earl of Arundel* (Cambridge: Cambridge University Press, 1921), 504–5, David Thomson, Letter to Earl of Arundel, July 1, 1625.

19. Thornton, *Landing at Cape Ann*, 43.

20. Hubbard, *General History*, 111.

21. Mark Kurlansky, *Cod* (New York: Penguin Books, 1998), 22.

22. Ibid., 27–28.

23. Ibid., 48–49

24. Mark Kurlansky, *Salt* (New York: Penguin Books, 2002), 110.

25. Ibid., 182.

26. Ibid., 132.

27. Kurlansky, *Cod*, 28–29.

28 Canadian Encyclopedia, "Red Bay Archaeological Site," http://www.thecanadianencyclopedia.ca.

29. Hubbard, *General History*, 10.

30. Henry Otis Thayer, *The Sagadahoc Colony* (Gorges Society, 1892), 43–44.

31. Ibid., 72.

32. Charles Knowles Bolton, *The Real Founders of New England* (Boston: F.W. Faxon Co., 1929), 26.

33. Ibid., 11–13.

34. Jack Dempsey, *Good News from New England and Other Writings on the Killings at the Weymouth Colony*, (Scituate, MA: Digital Scanning, 2001), 92

35. Bolton, *Real Founders of New England*, 11–13.

36. Ibid., 14.

37. William Bradford, *Of Plymouth Plantation, 1620–1647* (New York: Modern Library College, 1981), 227–28.

3. New England Before Salem

38. Thornton, *Landing at Cape Ann*, 1.

39. Ibid., 4–5.

40. Encyclopedia Virginia, "The First Charter of Virginia, 1606," https://encyclopediavirginia.org.

41. Thayer, *Sagadahoc Colony*.

42. Daniel Neal, *History of the Puritans or Protestant Nonconformists from the Reformation in 1517 to the Revolution in 1688* (New York: Harper & Brothers, 1844), 148.

43. Ibid., 149–50.

44. Bradford, *Of Plymouth Plantation*.

45. Ibid., 41–42

46. Ibid., 39.

47 Pilgrim Hall Museum, "Pierce Patent," www.pilgrimhallmuseum.org.

48. Thornton, *Landing at Cape Ann*, 14.

49. "Dorchester Company," http://www.encyclopedia.com/doc/1G2-3401801263.html.

50. Plymouth Colony timeline, http://worldhistoryproject.org/topics/plymouth-colony.

51. Bradford, *Of Plymouth Plantation*, 109–22.

52. Hubbard, *General History*, 73.

53. Virtual Jamestown, www.virtualjamestown.org.

54. Hubbard, *General History*, 77.

55. Virtual Jamestown, www.virtualjamestown.org.

56. Bradford, *Of Plymouth Plantation*, 128–29.

57. Dempsey, *Good News from New England*, 88–89.

58. Ibid., 47.

59. Ibid., 42–51.

60. Hubbard, *General History*, 78.

61. Dempsey, *Good News from New England*, 24.

4. Roger Conant and the Salt Trade of Seventeenth-Century London

62. Shipton, *Roger Conant*, 3.

63. Ibid., 110.

64. Ibid., 156.

65. Ibid., 8.

66. John Stevens Watson, *A History of the Salters Company* (Oxford University Press, 1964): 16–18.

67. Ibid., 42–43

68. Ibid., 18.

69. Ibid., 66–67

70. Ibid., 68.

71. Ibid., 39.

72. Ibid., 46–47

73. The Salters' Company, http://www.salters.co.uk/.

74. David Hume, *A History of England from Julius Caesar to the Revolution of 1688* (Edinburgh: Printed by Hamilton, Balfour and Neill, 1754), chapter 48.

75. Shipton, *Roger Conant*, 10–11.

76. Ibid., 12.

77. Bradford, *Of Plymouth Plantation*, 140.

78. Kurlansky, *Salt*, 209.

79. Shipton, *Roger Conant*.

80. David Lindsay, *Mayflower Bastard: A Stranger Among the Pilgrims* (New York: Thomas Dunne Books, 2002), 183.

81. Kurlansky, *Salt*, 2002.

82. Lindsay, *Mayflower Bastard*.

83. Bradford, *Of Plymouth Plantation*, 162–63.

5. Pilgrims versus Strangers

84. Thornton, *Landing at Cape Ann*, 36.
85. Bradford, *Of Plymouth Plantation*, 165
86. Ibid., 167.
87. Ibid., 167–76.
88. Ibid., 168.
89. Ibid., 168–69.
90. Ibid., 183.
91. Ibid., 185.
92. Ibid., 187.
93. Ibid., 184.

6. A New Colony Established and a Civil War Averted

94. Thornton, *Landing at Cape Ann*, 36.
95. Ibid., 37–38.
96. Ibid., 41–42.
97. Ibid., 40–41.
98. Ibid., 44.
99. Hubbard, *General History*, 107.
100. Thornton, *Landing at Cape Ann*, 45.
101. Hervey, *Life and Correspondence of Thomas Howard*, 504–5, David Thomson, Letter to Earl of Arundel, July 1, 1625.
102. Hubbard, *General History*, 111.
103. Bradford, *Of Plymouth Plantation*, 189.
104. William Bradford, letter to the Right and Honorable His Majesty's Council on New England, June 28th 1625.
105. Ibid.
106. Bradford, *Of Plymouth Plantation*, 199.

7. Failure and Opportunity

107. Reverend John White, "The Planter's Plea," 1630, Digital Public Library of America, https://dp.la.
108. Saville, *Champlain and His Landings*, 459.
109. Hubbard, *General History*, 107–8.
110. Joseph Felt, *The Annals of Salem* (James Munroe and Co., 1845), 38.
111. Thornton, *Landing at Cape Ann*, 49–50.
112. Hubbard, *General History*, 107.
113. Ibid., 108.
114. Shipton, *Roger Conant*, 60.
115. Felt, *Annals of Salem*, 21.

8. Becoming Salem

116. James Duncan Phillips, *Salem in the 17ᵗʰ Century* (New York: Riverdale Press, 1933), 39–40.

117. Ibid., 30–31.

118. Ibid., 48–49.

119. White, "Planters Plea."

120. Ibid.

121. Alexander Young, *The Chronicles of the First Planters of the Colony of Massachusetts Bay* (Boston: Charles Little & James Brown, 1847), 146–47

122. Ibid., 167–68.

123 Charles Moses Endicott, *Memoir of John Endecott, First Governor of the Colony of Massachusetts Bay* (Printed at the Salem Observer Office, 1817), 20.

124. Shipton, *Roger Conant*, 79.

125. Phillips, *Salem in the 17ᵗʰ Century*, 42.

126. Shipton, *Roger Conant*, 157

127. Endicott, *Memoir of John Endecott*, 25

128. Reverend Francis Higginson, *New-Englands Plantation, with the Sea Journal and Other Writings* (Essex Book Club, 1908).

9. The First Half Century

129. Bradford, *Of Plymouth Plantation*, 226–27.

130. C.H. Webber and W.S. Nevins, *Old Naumkeag: A Historical Sketch of the City of Salem* (Salem, MA: AA Smith & Co Publishers, 1877) 88.

131. Phillips, *Salem in the 17ᵗʰ Century*, 44.

132. Shipton, *Roger Conant*, 105.

133. Ibid., 101–13.

134. Ibid., 157.

INDEX

A

Agawam 25, 66, 67, 115, 132
Algonquin 25, 28, 98, 128
Argoll, Sir Sam 58

B

Balch, John 31, 109
Basque people 37, 114
Bradford, William 11, 31, 45, 52, 53,
        54, 62, 65, 66, 67, 68, 83, 84, 86,
        87, 88, 89, 90, 91, 92, 93, 98, 99,
        100, 102, 103, 109, 121, 129
Brewster, William 86
Bristol, UK 34, 35, 39
Budleigh, UK 39

C

Cape Ann 14, 16, 17, 20, 21, 23, 28,
        29, 30, 31, 34, 37, 41, 58, 59, 68,
        84, 85, 93, 94, 95, 96, 97, 98, 99,
        102, 103, 106, 107, 108, 109,
        111, 113, 114, 115, 119, 120,
        121, 124, 125, 131, 132, 134
Cape Ann Colony 17, 28, 31, 32, 46,
        54, 93, 95, 96, 99, 100, 101,
        103, 104, 105, 106, 107, 108,
        109, 110, 111, 114, 117, 118,
        119, 120, 123, 128, 130
Cape Cod 16, 23, 32, 56, 91, 131
Cartier, Jacques 37
Champlain, Samuel de 14, 16, 20,
        25, 106
cod 29, 30, 31, 32, 34, 35, 36, 37, 39,
        40, 42, 43, 45, 69, 81, 82, 99,
        100, 105, 106, 112, 117, 131
Conant, Roger 32, 46, 65, 67, 68, 69,
        70, 71, 72, 76, 77, 78, 79, 80,
        81, 83, 84, 85, 88, 90, 91, 92,
        96, 97, 98, 99, 101, 102, 106,
        107, 108, 109, 110, 111, 112,
        113, 114, 115, 117, 118, 119,
        120, 121, 123, 125, 126, 128,
        131, 132, 133, 134
Conant, Sarah 32, 80, 84, 96
Council of New England 59, 103,
        104, 119

D

Damariscove Island 40, 44, 65, 84
Devonshire 68, 69
Devon, UK 39, 69, 97

Dogtown 106
Dorchester Company 20, 23, 31, 59,
    93, 96, 97, 98, 99, 102, 104,
    105, 106, 108, 109, 113, 117,
    119, 121, 124

F

First Church Salem 69, 130, 133
First Parish Beverly 69, 133
Fishmongers Guild 75

G

Grand Banks 39
Gulf of Maine 39, 40

H

Hobbamock 62, 63

I

Ipswich 65, 66, 101, 114

J

Jamestown Colony 49, 60, 61, 118

K

Kennebec People 25
Kennebec River 49

L

Levett, Admiral Christopher 93, 94,
    104
Leyden, Holland 50, 87
London Adventurers 54, 55, 57, 58, 59
London Council 48, 50

M

Maine 14, 58, 62, 65, 84, 110, 115,
    131
Manchester, Massachusetts 20, 24, 83
Marblehead, Massachusetts 8, 20

Massachusett People 23, 25, 26, 28,
    61, 62, 63, 65, 66, 67, 98, 114,
    116, 126, 127, 132
Massachusetts Bay Colony 30, 102,
    109, 119, 120, 121, 123, 126,
    128, 129, 132
Massasoit 62
maypole 44, 45, 70, 90, 129, 130
Merrymont 116
Mi'kmaq People 25
Misery Island 107
Monhegan Island 38, 40, 41, 44, 49,
    62, 65
Morton, Thomas 22, 65, 85, 126,
    129, 130
Mount Wollaston (Merrymount) 129,
    130
Mourt's Relation 22

N

Nantasket 31, 41, 46, 85, 88, 90, 96
Narragansett Bay 13
Narragansett People 23, 28, 132
Naumkeag 17, 26, 27, 28, 98, 108,
    109, 110, 111, 113, 114, 115,
    117, 119, 121, 123, 125, 126,
    127, 128, 130, 134
Newfoundland 39, 40, 81

O

Oldham, John 85, 86, 87, 88, 89, 90,
    91, 92, 97, 102, 109, 132

P

Pierce Patent (first) 55
Pierce Patent (second) 57, 58
Piscataqua 46, 129
Plymouth Colony 46, 50, 52, 54, 55,
    56, 58, 59, 60, 61, 62, 63, 65,
    67, 83, 84, 85, 87, 89, 90, 92,
    93, 95, 96, 97, 98, 99, 100, 102,
    103, 104, 105, 108, 109, 110,

ABOUT THE AUTHOR

Author Benjamin Shallop's lifelong love of history began during his childhood in Salem, Massachusetts. Over the years, he has worked in the Florida Park Service, in education and as a community and labor organizer. As a labor organizer, he traveled extensively throughout the United States and worked closely with packinghouse workers, retail workers, food service workers and teachers. Throughout his travels, he would always look to the local history of the community he found himself in for inspiration. It is this working-class perspective that he brings to his history of the early settlement of Salem. In 2008, he moved back to Salem and began to rediscover the history that had initially inspired his love of learning as a child. Today, Mr. Shallop works as a union representative in the growing Massachusetts film industry and is an active member in several civic organizations in Salem.